Psychology in Teacher Preparation

edited by John Herbert and David P. Ausubel

MONOGRAPH SERIES NO. 5
THE ONTARIO INSTITUTE FOR STUDIES IN EDUCATION

THE ONTARIO INSTITUTE FOR STUDIES IN EDUCATION is a college chartered
by an Act of the Ontario Legislature in June, 1965. Its purpose is to study
matters and problems relating to education; to disseminate the results of and
assist in the implementation of the findings of educational studies; and to expand
graduate instruction in education. The Institute is affiliated with the
University of Toronto for degree-granting purposes.

We should like to thank the psychologists and teacher-preparation
staff members, too many for their names to be listed here, who made helpful
comments to the text of this collection.

We should also like to thank June Armstrong, conference secretary,
for her work on the pamphlet containing the recorders' reports, Ruth Sims
for her summary of the recorders' reports, and Barry Hemmings for
assembling the biographies of the authors.

Contents

Foreword

I know of no other aspect of teacher preparation more significant to us in Ontario at this stage of our development than the potential contribution of psychology to the professional education of teachers. We are in the process of making drastic changes: the emergency summer programs for the preparation of secondary school teachers have been terminated; the one-year post-high school program of our teachers colleges is to be discontinued, and the programs of preparation for elementary school teachers incorporated into the university structure; and steps have been taken to introduce a Master of Arts in Teaching Program, at present on a very limited scale.

Clearly, we are at one of those critical periods in our educational history when major changes either have been or will be introduced in teacher education. I would like to congratulate the staff of our two Departments directly concerned with the planning of this publication, Curriculum and Applied Psychology, for recognizing this opportunity, and for the wisdom they have shown in inviting as contributors distinguished scholars and practitioners from other provinces of Canada and from major institutions in the United States. I wish to thank those from other institutions who agreed to come to the International Conference on Psychology in the Teacher-Preparation Curriculum (April 4-6, 1968) held at The Ontario Institute for Studies in Education, Toronto. It was during this invitational conference that most of the following papers were originally presented. Not only do we have many problems in common with our colleagues in the United States and in Britain; but obviously, we in Ontario have much to learn from studies and experiences in other jurisdictions. Of course, we hope for a more effective component of psychology in teacher-preparation programs, but the first steps must include an exchange of ideas, an examination of current problems and progress, and probably the formulation of proposals for joint research and development projects which would ensure the further progress desired. In terms of our own tasks and priorities as an Institute, of course, nothing could be more fitting and encouraging — research and development being two of our three major functions.

We have had in this province a long and honorable history of teacher preparation. I must admit to the conviction, however, that in recent decades we have tended to cling rather tenaciously to traditional programs, and continued to do so until the past few years. Our district councils were authorized to establish "model schools" as early as 1843, and the first provincial normal school for the preparation of elementary school teachers was established in 1847. (Egerton Ryerson, the superintendent of education, based it on a combined Irish-German model.) Many attempts were made to provide preparation for secondary school teachers (grammar school teachers, as they were then known). A model grammar school opened in 1858, but this was short-lived. In 1885 training began in a selected group of collegiate institutes, and was replaced in 1890 by programs in a provincial School of Pedagogy established in Toronto. In 1897 the school was moved to Hamilton, and renamed the Ontario Normal College. Faculties of education were founded in Toronto in 1907 and in Kingston the following year. These were eventually discontinued, and the Ontario College of Education was opened at Toronto in 1920. In the last four years, two more colleges of education have been established in Ontario. Now, I suppose we may complete the cycle and return to faculties of education in many universities!

It would be of some interest to trace the influence of the view held in secondary school circles of those early days, and still widely held in some university circles today, that if a man knew his subject then obviously he could teach competently without any professional preparation. The emphasis in teacher education programs has always been on specific methods of teaching subjects; indeed, some educators held the view that a person trained to teach in this way could teach any subject to any student. Nevertheless, even in my day the teacher-training program had some general courses, of which psychology frequently, if not invariably, was one. I can still vividly remember the frustrations associated with the course I took in psychology in normal school; the title of the textbook was "General Psychology," and it included everything from physiology to abnormal psychology. The course was taught from the textbook by the master responsible for teaching methods in one of the subjects (I believe it was Art). The course had little relevance to the problems of teaching children, and probably even less resemblance to psychology, but as students we learned to survive by ignoring the content, except for examination purposes.

I must admit that I was somewhat taken aback by the repeated references in the background papers to the fact that, even today, many eminent scholars hold that the traditional psychology courses are largely irrelevant to teaching, possibly even harmful. I also observed, however, that some of you, as the paper on the proposed program at Harvard indicates, believe a suitable presentation and use of current psychological knowledge can be of considerable assistance to teachers. In terms of future developments, I was encouraged by the thesis advanced by David Ausubel, that "educational psychology is that special branch of psychology concerned with the nature, conditions, outcomes, and evaluation of school learning and retention," by his emphasis on *classroom* learning and the need to take into account "both the kinds of learning that occur in the classroom as well as the salient characteristics of the learner," by his prediction of the major trends likely to emerge in the coming decade, and by his conviction that the new discipline of educational psychology can be organized on the basis of a rational classification of learning variables involved in the classroom instruction. John Herbert, in his proposal for the development of an analytic-applied psychology course for teacher-preparation programs, points out that "professors of psychology and curriculum departments could work with teacher educators in an effective formulation and evaluation of a program to help teachers in their increasingly complex work."

Our goal, as I understand it, is to ensure that current psychological knowledge can help the teacher know the child and understand how learning takes place in the classroom, to see why successful teachers teach the way they do, and to discover how the new technologies can be used most effectively.

In this province, and in other jurisdictions, we are attempting to cast off the shackles of the lockstep graded school system and move toward individualized instruction and the education of each child according to his needs and capacities. I would suggest that the extent to which we can be successful in these efforts will be determined in large measure by the degree to which we can achieve the goals of this publication. More depends on these deliberations and findings than perhaps most of us realize, in our schools and society as well as in our teacher-preparation programs.

As a final comment, may I remind you that this is not merely an academic exercise. There is a real urgency in the matter, as we change our programs and continue to prepare thousands of teachers to teach new courses in new kinds of schools. If psychologists, in cooperation with teacher educators, can develop programs that will provide the assistance and knowledge referred to above, then psychology will merit a high priority in any teacher-preparation program.

R. W. B. JACKSON
Director
The Ontario Institute for Studies in Education

THE PROBLEM

Positions and Common Ground

John Herbert

Educational psychology as it is now taught in teacher-preparation programs ought to be changed drastically and soon. Such is the opinion of the authors, all professors of educational psychology in universities or colleges in Canada, the United States, and Britain, represented in this collection. Such, too, is the opinion of the teachers, teacher educators, and educational psychologists who attended the Invitational Conference. Perhaps not everyone present would have agreed with John Macdonald when he called the typical educational psychology course "a curious mish-mash," or with Floyd Robinson when he described the preparation of teachers in psychology as useless, irrelevant, vague, or misleading, and a "pitiful caricature of good advice," or with David Ausubel when he summed up the content of the usual textbook as "a superficial, ill-digested and typically disjointed and watered-down miscellany." Nevertheless there was general agreement among the hundred distinguished delegates to the conference that teachers are receiving an entirely inadequate preparation in psychology.

Surprisingly few attempts are being made to improve a situation that so many deprecate. At Harvard, Stanford, and Alberta, as Belanger, McDonald, and Corman report, new programs are being developed for beginning teachers. But these experiments, and others like them, are relatively isolated and unsupported. At present there is no major curriculum project in educational psychology at all comparable to those which have been undertaken in other subjects, and no large-scale effort to effect changes in teacher preparation has to my knowledge been initiated by educational psychologists.

Why should this be so? The authors of the papers in this collection identify a number of barriers to progress. Some argue that in the present state of the discipline educational psychology has little to teach teachers, and that reform of the curriculum must therefore wait for reform of the discipline. Others believe that the teaching of psychology can be improved only if teacher-preparation programs as a whole are expanded, extended, and upgraded. Still others contend that the present conception of the nature and purpose of the school and the power structure of the school system must be changed before educational psychology can contribute effectively. Finally, some think

1

that in the future educational psychology will become irrelevant to the work of teachers because their relation to the curriculum will be altered by technological changes which may even go far enough to eliminate their pedagogical functions altogether.

The position one takes on each of these issues determines the way one identifies and ranks the tasks educational psychologists will have to undertake before substantial progress can be expected. The first step is therefore clarification of the main positions and of their implications for action.

If, for example, further progress depends upon reform of the discipline, several tasks must be given high priority. One would be to eliminate from courses and programs in educational psychology for teachers those irrelevant portions of general and clinical psychology, which now merely pad the textbooks and sustain the professional self-esteem of those psychologists. The task of selection comes next. But several major obstacles must first be overcome — among which are the absence of a body of research with known relevance to schooling, teaching, and learning; and the shortage of competent educational psychologists willing to perform the needed work. As Ausubel points out, educational psychologists have tended "to extrapolate findings from basic science to pedagogical problems without conducting the additional research necessary to bridge the gap between the two levels of generality involved."

University departments of educational psychology have the primary responsibility for improving the training and orientation of research workers in the field. If improvements are to be made, however, the schools will have to cooperate by welcoming educational psychologists and providing facilities for them. While some school districts have already participated irregularly in designing and conducting research projects, there is a great need for more consistent and widespread collaboration, which might well extend to joint management of projects and experimental schools or classes. The first step would be for educational psychologists, representatives of school systems and teachers' associations, and those responsible for teacher-preparation programs to agree on suitable conditions for the regular encouragement of research. The members of the groups who participated in the conference demonstrated their willingness to work toward such cooperation.

Some speakers at the conference suggested that a faulty conception of the discipline is also partly to blame for another barrier to progress: the nature of the present teacher-preparation programs. Frederick McDonald maintains that we have failed to distinguish clearly educational psychology as a discipline (a research-based field of knowledge important to anyone interested in education) from the problems of how to develop and organize teacher-training programs and of how to train teachers to use psychology. For those who teach educational psychology in teacher-preparation programs, one means of improving teacher preparation might be to conduct research on what and how much their students are able to learn at various stages of their training, and on the nature and effectiveness of training procedures other than the giving of courses.

But a more direct line of attack also seems possible. Some participants in the discussion groups at the conference suggested that part of the difficulty is simply that teacher-preparation programs are so brief and so deficient in staff and facilities that there is little that psychologists can do except to pass out a few prescriptions for survival and our best wishes. If this is so, should not educational psychologists strongly advise those responsible for planning programs and allocating resources that educational psychology has more to contribute and that they ought to change their policies?

Another issue is the question of the way in which existing or potential resources can be used most effectively. Some speakers took the position that under present circumstances psychological knowledge cannot be used efficiently to change teacher-preparation programs. Stephens, for example, suggested that as a result of background factors in the culture, teachers already teach well enough to make significant improvement by deliberate training unlikely without a disproportionate expenditure of resources, or at least that any improvement would be too small to be detectable to researchers. Robinson also believes that it would be uneconomic to improve the psychological training of teachers, but for a different reason. He believes that in the present power structure, teachers are not permitted to make decisions of the kind to which educational research is applicable. He would provide improved training for those specialists, notably methodologists and curriculum developers, whose decisions he believes have the maximum actual or potential effect on the classroom.

Given the models of schools presented in these two papers, teacher training may not be a suitable concern of educational psychologists. Other speakers, however, denied that these models accurately represent contemporary reality, and most of the participants in the conference were of the opinion that changes in today's society are so extensive and powerful that teachers and schools must either choose to change or be forced to change. At times, indeed, the paleontological and evolutionary metaphors used by the speakers were evocative of the last stand of a dying species against inevitable ecological and technological changes. Thus Birch spoke of the view that education has "fossilized in its present North American model." Stephens claimed that schooling is entirely dominated by social and behavioral traits dating from an early stage of human evolution. John Macdonald also agreed that our schools are "relatively primitive institution[s]." Frederick McDonald declared that unless teachers have a non-replicable function, we in teacher education "are simply polishing the bones of the dinosaur . . . and might more appropriately call ourselves paleontologists." Corman also expressed doubt for the survival of teachers in the new world created by the coming cataclysm and by the technology he described as the psychologists' atom bomb for teachers.

While most of the contributors speak of changes in the schools, they do not agree in their predictions. Birch, on the one hand, asserts: "The first outcome of this change will, I predict, be the emergence of a much more professional teaching body in the schools. The teachers will demand greater responsibility and control over all aspects of their work. At the same time they will demand higher professional standards of their members. The first casualty will be the curriculum builder, for responsibility for what is taught, and how, will rest firmly with the school principal and his staff." Corman and Robinson, on the other hand, see the increasing powerlessness of teachers as a major feature of the new model of the schools. They believe that in the future decisions about what to teach and when will be made by specialists who will prepare materials for teachers to administer. Corman predicts that experts who administer the expensive educational technology will commit the schools totally through their purchases, and that unless teachers can make themselves independent as specialists in human relationships, their only freedom in the future will be freedom to serve the machine.

As a group, however, the delegates foresaw a renovation of the schools rather than their extinction. The focal point of controversy seemed to lie in their differing views on the future role of the teacher in the school, which partly depends upon the experience and expectations of teachers now in the schools. Ausubel clearly has a high conception of their work: "[The teachers] must generate interest in the subject matter, inspire commitment to learning, motivate pupils, and help induce realistic aspirations for educational achievement. He must decide what is important for pupils to learn, ascertain what learning they are ready for, pace instruction properly, and decide on the appropriate size and difficulty level of learning tasks." This is clearly very different from the conception of the typical teacher presented by some other speakers who saw him as a subject specialist made anxious and incompetent by the brevity and low quality of his preparation in his subject, or as a semi-professional of mediocre capacity and aspirations who craves ready-made dogma and packaged knowledge. If these different conceptions of the teacher are based on differences among teachers, then perhaps the structure of the profession and of school staffs ought to be changed to give appropriate functions to teachers of varying levels of ability. Doubtless, educational psychology could contribute to this reform. It may be, however, as Frederick McDonald suggests, that the different conceptions of the teacher actually represent progressive phases of development, and that with improved training procedures many could develop a sophisticated and creative adaptation to the complex environment of the classroom.

The emergence of such fundamental differences constitutes one of the contributions of the present collection. Fruitful debate must necessarily come before any cooperative effort to effect change; such a debate would require a clear definition of the issues that divide those who must act. Clear definitions of fundamental issues cannot be formulated until those who are divided find sufficient common ground to be able to listen to another's arguments.

Participants in the conference found such common ground where many had not expected to find it. Teachers and teacher-preparation staff members seem increasingly willing to work with psychologists, and psychologists increasingly willing to accept one another's theoretical positions. No one among the educational psychologists at the conference suggested a return to the laboratory or to questions of general theory. All were intensely interested in the quality of classroom teaching and learning and consequently, could argue with one another and with teachers and teacher educators about ways in which educational psychology might influence what goes on in the classroom. Perhaps what lies behind the universal criticism of current offerings in educational psychology for teachers is an acute sense of the gulf between what is expected and what is realized.

Is There a Discipline of Educational Psychology?[1]

David P. Ausubel

"Is there such a discipline as educational psychology?" is certainly not an irrelevant or irreverent question. On the contrary, it follows very pertinently if one examines many textbooks of educational psychology that were written during the past thirty years. In fact, judging from the conception of educational psychology — as a superficial, ill-digested, and typically disjointed and watered-down miscellany of general psychology, learning theory, developmental psychology, social psychology, psychological measurement, psychology of adjustment, mental hygiene, client-centered counseling and child-centered education put forward by these textbooks — one would be hard put not to give a negative answer to the question raised by the title of this paper.

Definition of the field

My thesis, in brief, is that educational psychology is that special branch of psychology concerned with the nature, conditions, outcomes, and evaluation of school learning and retention. As such, the subject matter of educational psychology consists primarily of the theory of meaningful learning and the retention and the influence of all significant variables — cognitive, developmental, affective, motivational, personality, and social — on school learning outcomes: particularly the influence of those variables that are manipulable by the teacher, the curriculum developer, the programmed instruction specialist, the educational technologist, the school psychologist or guidance counselor, the educational administrator, or society at large.

Psychology versus educational psychology

Since both psychology and educational psychology deal with the problem of learning, how can we distinguish between the theoretical and research interests of each discipline in this area? As an applied science, educational psychology is not concerned with general laws of learning *per se*, but only with those properties of learning that can be related to efficacious ways of *deliberately* effecting stable cognitive changes that have social value (Ausubel, 1953).

1. This paper was first given at a Symposium on Research Opportunities and Coming Changes in the Teaching of Psychology to Teachers at the Annual Meeting of the American Educational Research Association and has appeared in *Psychology in the Schools*, 1969 (July), **6** (3), 232-244.

Education, therefore, refers to guided or manipulated learning directed toward specific practical ends. These ends may be defined as the long-term acquisition of stable bodies of knowledge and of the capacities needed for acquiring such knowledge.

The psychologist's interest in learning, on the other hand, is much more general. Many aspects of learning, other than the efficient achievement of the above-designated competencies and capacities for growth in a directed context, concern him. More typically, he investigates the nature of simple, fragmentary, or short-term learning experiences, which are presumably more representative of learning in general, rather than the kinds of long-term learning involved in assimilating extensive and organized bodies of knowledge.

The following kinds of learning problems, therefore, are particularly indigenous to psychoeducational research: (*a*) discovery of the *nature* of those aspects of the learning process affecting the acquisition and long-term retention of organized bodies of knowledge in the learner; (*b*) discovery of ways to achieve long-range improvement of learning and problem-solving capacities; (*c*) discovery of which cognitive and personality characteristics of the learner, and of which interpersonal and social aspects of the learning environment affect subject-matter learning outcomes, motivation for learning, and ways of assimilating school material; and (*d*) discovery of appropriate and maximally efficient ways of organizing and presenting learning materials and of deliberately motivating and directing learning toward specific goals.

Another way of epitomizing the difference between the two disciplines is to say that general aspects of learning are a concern of the psychologist, whereas classroom learning, that is, deliberately guided learning of subject matter in a particular social context, is the special province of the educational psychologist. The subject matter of educational psychology, therefore, can be inferred directly from the problems facing the classroom teacher. The latter must generate interest in subject matter, inspire commitment to learning, motivate pupils, and help induce realistic aspirations for educational achievement. He must decide what is important for pupils to learn, ascertain what learning they are ready for, pace instruction properly, and decide on the appropriate size and difficulty level of learning tasks. He is expected to organize subject matter expeditiously, present materials clearly, simplify learning tasks at initial stages of mastery, and integrate current and past learnings. It is his responsibility to arrange practice schedules and reviews, to confirm, clarify, and correct, to ask critical questions, to provide suitable rewards, to evaluate learning and development, and where feasible, to promote discovery learning and problem-solving ability. Finally, since he is concerned with teaching groups of students in a social environment, he must grapple with problems of group instruction, individualization, communication, and discipline.

Thus the scope of educational psychology as an applied science is exceedingly broad, and the potential rewards it offers in terms of the social value of facilitating the subject-matter learning of pupils are proportionately great.

In what sense is educational psychology an "applied" discipline?

Few persons would take issue with the proposition that education is an applied or engineering science. It is an applied science[2] because it is concerned with the realization of certain practical ends that have social value. The precise nature of these ends is highly controversial in terms of both substance and relative emphasis. To some individuals the function of education is to transmit the ideology of the culture, a core of knowledge, and intellectual skills. To others, education is primarily concerned with the optimal development of potentiality for growth and achievement — not only with respect to cognitive abilities, but also with respect to personality goals and adjustment. Disagreement regarding ends, however, neither removes education from the category of science nor makes it any less of an applied branch of knowledge. It might be mentioned in passing that automobile engineers are also not entirely agreed as to the characteristics of the "ideal" car; and physicians disagree violently in their definition of health.

Regardless of the ends it chooses to adopt, an applied discipline becomes a science only when it seeks to ground proposed means to ends on propositions that can be validated empirically. The operations involved in such an undertaking are commonly subsumed under the term "research." The question under discussion here relates to the nature of research in applied science or, more specifically, in education. Is educational research a field in its own right, with theoretical problems and a methodology of its own, or does it merely involve the operation of applying knowledge from "pure" scientific disciplines to practical problems of pedagogy?

Despite the fact that education is an applied science, educational psychologists have manifested a marked tendency to extrapolate uncritically from research findings of laboratory studies of simplified learning situations to the classroom learning environment. This tendency reflects the fascination which many research workers feel for the "basic-science" approach to research in the applied sciences, as well as their concomitant failure to appreciate its inherent limitations. They argue that progress in educational psychology is made more rapidly by focusing indirectly on basic-science problems in general psychology than by trying to come to grips directly with the applied-science problems that are indigenous to the field. Spence (1959), for example, perceived classroom learning as much too complex to permit the discovery of general laws of learning and advocated a straightforward application of the laws of learning discovered in the laboratory to the classroom situation; he saw very little scope, however, for applying the latter laws to problems of educational practice. Melton (1959) and Hilgard (1964) take a more eclectic position. They would search for basic-science laws of learning in both labora-

---

2. The term "applied" is used here to distinguish between sciences which are oriented toward practical ends, as opposed to "basic" or "parent" sciences which do not have this orientation. "Applied" does not imply that the content of the practical disciplines consists of applications from the basic or parent disciplines. The *problems* rather than the *knowledge* of applied sciences are "applied."

tory and classroom contexts, and would leave to the educational technologist the task of conducting the research necessary for implementing these laws in actual classroom practice.

My position, in other words, is that the principles governing the nature and conditions of classroom learning can be discovered only through an applied type of research that actually takes into account both the kinds of learning that occur in the classroom and the salient characteristics of the learner. We cannot merely apply to classroom learning general basic-science laws that are derived from the laboratory study of qualitatively different and vastly simpler instances of learning. Most attempts to do so, as, for example, Mandler's (1962) attempt to explain complex cognitive functioning in terms of the laws of association, or Sheffield's (1961) recent explanation of the hierarchical learning of sequentially organized materials in terms of the principle of contiguous conditioning, are extremely tortuous.

Laws of classroom learning at an applied[3] level are needed by the educational technologist before he can hope to conduct the research preparatory to effect scientific changes in teaching practices. He can be aided further by principles of teaching which are intermediate in generality and prescriptiveness between laws of classroom learning and the technological problems that confront him. Contrary to Spence's (1959) contention, the greater complexity and number of determining variables involved in classroom learning does not preclude the possibility of discovering precise laws with wide applicability from one educational situation to another. It simply means that such research demands the experimental ingenuity and sophisticated use of modern techniques of research design.

The basic science versus the applied science approach

Three different kinds of research orientations have been adopted by those who are concerned with scientific progress in applied disciplines such as medicine and education: (*a*) basic-science research, (*b*) extrapolated research in the basic sciences, and (*c*) applied research (Ausubel, 1953).

The basic-science research approach is predicated on the very defensible proposition that applied sciences are ultimately related to knowledge in the sciences on which they are based. It can be demonstrated convincingly, for example, that progress in medicine is intimately related to progress in general biochemistry and bacteriology; progress in engineering to progress in physics and chemistry; and progress in education to advances in general psychology, statistics, and sociology. However, two important sets of qualifications have to be placed on the value of basic-science research for the applied sciences: qualifications of purpose or relevance and qualifications of the level of applicability.

---

3. These laws are just as "basic" as basic-science laws. The terms "basic" and "applied" refer to the distinction between basic ("pure," "parent") and applied ("practical") sciences made earlier. "Basic" does not mean "fundamental." In the latter sense, applied research is just as basic for its distinctive domain as research in the pure sciences is for its domain.

By definition, basic-science research is concerned with the discovery of general laws of physical, biological, psychological, and sociological phenomenology as an end in itself. Researchers in these fields would not object to having their findings applied to practical problems that have social value. In fact, there is reason to believe that they are motivated to some extent by this consideration. But the design of basic-science research bears no intended relation whatsoever to problems in the applied disciplines; its aim is solely to advance knowledge. Ultimately, of course, such knowledge is applicable in a very broad sense to practical problems; but since the research design is not oriented to the solution of these problems, this applicability is apt to be quite indirect and unsystematic, and relevant only over a time span too long to be meaningful to the immediate needs of the applied disciplines.

The second qualification has to do with the level at which findings in the basic-sciences can be applied once their relevance has been established. It should be self-evident that such findings exhibit a much higher level of generality than the problems to which they can be applied. At the level of application, specific ends and conditions are added that demand *additional* research to indicate the precise way in which the general law operates in the specific case. That is, the applicability of general principles to specific problems is *not given* in the statement of the general principle, but must be explicitly worked out for each individual problem. Knowledge about nuclear fission, for example, does not tell us how to make an atomic bomb or an atomic-powered airplane.

In fields such as education, the problem of generality is further complicated by the fact that practical problems often exist at higher levels of complexity (with respect to the order of phenomenology involved) than do the basic-science findings that require application. New variables are added which may *qualitatively* alter the general principles from the basic science so that at the applied level they have substrate validity but lack explanatory or predictive value. For example, antibiotic reactions that take place in test tubes do not necessarily take place in living systems, and methods of rote learning that children use in mastering lists of nonsense syllables in the laboratory do not necessarily correspond to methods of learning they use in acquiring a meaningful grasp of subject matter in the classroom.

The basic-science approach in educational research, therefore, is subject to many serious disadvantages. Its relevance is too remote and indirect because it is not oriented toward solving educational problems. Its findings, if relevant, are applicable only if much additional research is performed to translate general principles into the more specific form pertinent to the task-specialized and more complex context of pedagogy.

These limitations would not be so serious if they were acknowledged. It would be defensible for educational institutions to set aside a small portion of their research funds for basic-science research as a long-term investment. But since the limitations of this approach are *not* generally appreciated, some bureaus of educational research confidently invest their major resources in basic-science programs, and then complacently expect that the findings that emerge will be both relevant and applicable in their original form to educational problems.

Naïveté with respect to the immediate applicability of findings from the basic-science approach has led to very serious distortions in our knowledge of those pedagogical aspects of the psychology of learning. The psychology of learning that teachers study is based on findings that have been borrowed from general psychology wholesale without much attempt to test their applicability to the kinds of learning situations in classrooms. It would be a shocking situation indeed if a comparable procedure were practiced in medicine; that is, if physicians employed therapeutic techniques validated only *in vitro* or by animal experimentation.

The second approach taken up by research in the applied disciplines is based on the extrapolations from the basic sciences. Unlike pure basic-science research, this approach is oriented toward the solution of practical problems. It starts out by identifying significant problems in the applied field, and designs experiments to be solved on an analogous but highly simplified basic-science level. In this way it satisfies the important criterion of relevance, but must still contend with the problem of level of applicability. The rationale of this approach is that many practical problems are so complex that they must be reduced to simpler terms, and patterned after simpler models, before anyone can develop fruitful hypotheses leading to their solution. Once the problems are simplified, control and measurement become more manageable.

Extrapolations from the basic-science research may have genuine merit provided that the resulting research findings are regarded only as "leads" or hypotheses to be tested in the applied situation, rather than as definitive answers to problems in pedagogy. As has been noted, educational researchers have a tendency to extrapolate findings from basic science to pedagogical problems without conducting the additional research necessary to bridge the gap between the two levels of generality involved.

The third approach to educational research is the most relevant and direct of the three, yet ironically it is least used of all. When research is performed in relation to the actual problems of education, under the conditions in which they are to be found in practice, the problems of relevance and extrapolation do not arise.[4] Most rigorous research in applied disciplines other than education is conducted at this level. The research program of a hospital or medical school would be regarded as seriously unbalanced if most of its funds and efforts went into pure biochemical or bacteriological research instead of into applied and clinical research. The major responsibility for furthering research in those theoretical areas belongs to graduate departments of chemistry and

---

4. Applied research is also directed toward the discovery of *general* laws within the framework of its applied ends. The generalizations it discovers, therefore, exist at a different plane of generality than those of "basic" science research.

bacteriology. On the other hand, unless medical schools undertake to solve their own applied and clinical problems who else will? The same analogy obviously holds true for education.

Although applied research presents greater difficulties with respect to research design, control, and measurement, the rewards are correspondingly greater. Certainly these problems cannot be deliberately avoided. If other applied disciplines have been able to evolve satisfactory research methodologies, there is no reason why education cannot also do so. In fact, if any applied discipline with unique and distinctive problems of its own is to survive as a science it is obliged to do so.

Many of the better known generalizations in educational psychology — the principle of readiness, the effects of overlearning, the concrete-to-abstract trend in conceptualizing the environment — illustrate the pitfalls of the basic-science approach to educational research. They are interesting and potentially useful ideas to curriculum specialists and educational technologists, but are of little use to educational practice until they are particularized at an applied level. The prevailing lack of particularization damages the "image" of educational psychology insofar as it induces many beginning teachers to nurture unrealistic expectations about the current usefulness of these principles. Subsequently, after undergoing acute disillusionment, they may lose whatever confidence they originally had in the value of a psychological approach to educational problems.

The need for applied research in these areas is well illustrated by the principles of readiness. At present we can only speculate as to what curriculum sequences would look like if they took into account precise and detailed (but currently unavailable) research findings on readiness for the study of different subject areas, for different subareas and levels of difficulty within an area, and for different methods of teaching the same material. For example, because of the unpredictable specificity of readiness, as shown by the fact that four- and five-year-olds can profit from training in pitch but not in rhythm (Jersild and Bienstock, 1931, 1935), valid answers cannot be derived from logical extrapolation; they require meticulous empirical research in a school setting. The next step involves the development of teaching methods and materials appropriate for taking optimal advantage of existing degrees of readiness, and for increasing readiness wherever necessary and desirable. But because these research data are not generally available, except perhaps in reading, we can pay only lip service to principles of readiness in curriculum planning.

The basic-science-extrapolation approach, of course, has several very attractive methodological advantages in verbal learning experiments. First, by using nonsense syllables of equal meaninglessness, it is possible to work with additive units of equal difficulty. Second, by using relatively meaningless learning tasks, such as equated nonsense syllables, it is possible to eliminate, for the most part, the indeterminable influence of meaningful antecedent experience, which naturally varies from one individual to another. But it is precisely this interaction between new learning tasks and existing knowledge in the learner that is the distinctive feature of meaningful learning.

Thus, although the use of nonsense syllables doubtlessly adds methodological rigor to the study of learning, the very nature of the material limits the applicability of experimental findings to a type of short-term, discrete learning which is rare in both everyday situations and the classroom. Nevertheless, even though there are no *a priori* grounds for supposing that meaningful and non-meaningful learning and retention occur in the same way, the findings from rote-learning experiments have been commonly applied to meaningful learning situations. One cannot have one's cake and eat it too. If one chooses the particular kind of methodological rigor associated with the use of rote materials, one must also be satisfied with applying the findings from such experiments only to rote-learning tasks.

In conclusion, therefore, educational psychology is unequivocally an applied discipline, but it is not general psychology applied to educational problems any more than mechanical engineering is general physics applied to problems of designing machinery or medicine is general biology applied to problems of diagnosing, curing, and preventing human diseases. In the above applied disciplines, general laws from the parent discipline are not applied to practical problems; instead, separate bodies of applied theory exist that are just as basic as the theory underlying the parent disciplines but are stated at a lower level of generality and with more direct relevance for and applicability to the problems in their respective fields.

The particular properties of knowledge in the applied sciences have also been exaggerated. Such knowledge involves more than the technological application of generalizations from basic science to current practical problems. The applied sciences are also disciplines *in their own right*, with distinctive and relatively enduring bodies of theory and methodology that cannot be derived or extrapolated from the basic sciences to which they are related. It is simply not true that only knowledge of the basic sciences can be related to and organized around general principles. Each of the applied biological sciences (e.g., medicine and agronomy) possesses an independent body of general principles underlying the detailed knowledge in its field, in addition to being related in a more general way to basic principles in biology.

Theories of learning versus theories of teaching

Disillusionment regarding the relevance and usefulness of learning theory for educational practice has been responsible, in part, for the recent emergence of "theories of teaching" that are avowedly independent of theories of learning. The justification for such theories of teaching has been advanced on both historical and logical grounds.

The historical argument. Gage (1964) cites the historical record in his argument that theories of learning have had very little applicability to and influence on educational practice, whether in educational psychology textbooks, in courses devoted to teaching methods, or in the everyday operations of classroom teaching. He argues further that theories of learning are inherently irrelevant for problems of instruction, and should therefore be replaced by theories of teaching in dealing with such problems. For example, he states that:

> While theories of learning deal with the ways in which an organism learns, theories of teaching deal with the ways in which a person influences an organism to learn . . . . To satisfy the practical demands of education, theories of learning must be "stood on their head" so as to yield theories of teaching [pp. 268-269].

Actually, *both* of these arguments are based essentially on the historical failure of learning theory to provide a psychologically relevant basis for pedagogic practice. This undeniable shortcoming of learning theory is by no means a necessary or inherent limitation in its applicability to education. It is merely characteristic of the prevailing brand of school learning theory, which, in general, does not deal with the kind of learning that occurs in the classroom but with the extrapolations from the main body of laboratory learning theory. A realistic and scientifically viable theory of classroom learning, in contrast, would be primarily concerned with complex and meaningful types of verbal and symbolic learning that take place in school and similar learning environments, and also with giving a prominent place to those *manipulable* factors that affect it. There is, in other words, a very close relationship between knowing how a pupil learns and the manipulable variables influencing learning, on the one hand, and knowing what to do to help him learn better, on the other. By "teaching" we mean primarily the deliberate guidance of learning processes along lines suggested by relevant classroom learning theory. It would seem reasonable, therefore, that the discovery of the most effective methods of teaching would be inherently dependent upon and related to the status of learning theory.

Of course, only *general* principles of learning could be considered as part of classroom learning theory. The more applied and prescriptive aspects of pedagogy that are derived from these principles would constitute a theory of instruction and would continue to be taught in methods courses.

The logical argument. In contrast to Gage's historical argument, B. O. Smith (1960) presents a strictly logical rationale for formulating theories of teaching that are wholly independent of theories of learning. He bases his case on the propositions that learning and teaching are neither coextensive with nor inextricable from each other, and that a theory of learning cannot tell us how to teach.

First, Smith's insistence that learning and teaching are different and separately identifiable phenomena admittedly does more than belabor the obvious. It clears up the confusion implied in the statement that "if the child has not learned, the teacher has not taught," or else has taught incompetently. Teaching and learning are not coextensive, for teaching is only one of the conditions, and not a necessary or sufficient one, which may influence learning. Thus pupils can learn without being taught, that is, by teaching themselves; and even if teaching is manifestly competent, it does not necessarily lead to learning if the pupils concerned are inattentive, unmotivated, or cognitively unprepared.

Nevertheless, once these unwarranted inferences about the coextensiveness of learning and teaching are discarded, it is useful to focus on those aspects of teaching and learning that are related to each other. These relationships include the purposes, effects, and evaluation of teaching. Thus, although it is true that teaching is logically distinct from learning, and that what pupils learn can be analyzed independently of what they are taught, what would be the practical advantage of so doing? The facilitation of learning is the only proper end of teaching. We do not teach as an end in itself but only that pupils may learn; and even though the pupils' failure to learn does not necessarily indict the teacher, learning is still the only feasible measure of teaching merit. Further, as has been pointed out, teaching itself is effective only to the extent that it manipulates effectively those psychological variables that govern learning.

Second, even though a valid theory of learning cannot tell us how to teach, in a prescriptive sense, it does offer us general principles of teaching that can be formulated in terms of both intervening psychological processes and cause-effect relationships. It is largely from a theory of learning that we can develop defensible notions of how crucial factors in the learning-teaching situation can be most effectively manipulated. The only other possible approach is either to vary teaching factors at random or to rely on intuition. The latter approach is more time-consuming, and can only yield purely empirical laws that cannot be formulated in general terms with respect to the psychological conditions and relevant cognitive processes involved.

It is realized, of course, that an adequate theory of learning is necessary but does not provide a sufficient condition for the improvement of instruction. Valid principles of teaching, though necessarily based on relevant principles of learning, are not, as pointed out above, simple and direct applications of these principles. Laws of classroom learning merely provide the general direction for discovering effective teaching principles; they do not indicate *per se* what these principles are. The formulation of teaching principles requires much supplementary research that takes into account practical problems and new instructional variables not implicit in the learning principle. In other words, one can consider basic principles of teaching as applied derivatives of school learning theory; they are products of an engineering type of research and are based on such modifications of learning theory as are necessitated by the practical difficulties or the additional new variables involved in teaching.

As Smith (1960) asserts in *Critical Thinking*, simply by knowing "the cause of a phenomenon," one does not thereby acquire control of it "for practical ends [p. 87]." (For example, we can know the cause of a disease without knowing how to treat it, and we can treat a disease successfully without knowing its cause.) It is undeniable that many practical and useful inventions are made accidentally without any understanding of the explanatory principles and relevant variables involved. But who would advocate this as a deliberate research strategy? Ordinarily, scientists search for practical methods of control that can be related to general statements of relationship among the relevant variables involved. The superiority of this approach lies in the fact that methods of control that are relatable to general principles are not only understandable and interpretable, but more widely transferable to other practical problems. We could, for example, discover as an empirical fact that using teaching method X facilitates learning. But the practical value of such knowledge is quite limited. Would it not be preferable to formulate the research problem so that we could ascertain in what ways method X influences relevant psychological variables and intervening cognitive states in the course of facilitating learning, retention or problem-solving? It is an extreme waste of time and effort to search for more efficient methods of teaching that can be described only in terms of descriptive characteristics of the teaching act and cannot be related to laws of learning.

Finally, although knowledge of causation does not imply immediate discovery of control procedures, it does constitute a tremendous advantage in discovering them. For one thing, it narrows the field; for another, it enables one to try procedures that have proven successful in controlling related conditions. Knowing that tuberculosis was caused by a microorganism, for example, did not provide us immediately with a cure or a preventative. But it enabled us to try approaches such as vaccines, immune sera, antisepsis, quarantine, and chemotherapy that had been used successfully in treating other infectious diseases. In the same sense, knowledge of the cause of cancer would help immeasurably in discovering a cure, and knowledge of the nature and relevant variables involved in concept acquisition would be of invaluable assistance in devising effective methods of teaching concepts.

The decline of classroom learning theory

The serious decline in knowledge and theorizing about classroom learning that has taken place over the past fifty years, accompanied by the steady retreat of educational psychologists from the classroom, has not been without adequate cause. Much of this can be attributed to the scientific disrepute into which studies of classroom learning have fallen as a result of both glaring deficiencies in conceptualization and research design, and excessive concern with the improvement of narrowly conceived academic skills and techniques of instruction rather than with the discovery of more general principles affecting the improvement of classroom learning and instruction in *any* subject-matter field. The vast majority of studies in the field of classroom learning, after all, has been conducted by teachers and other nonprofessional research workers in education. In contrast, laboratory studies of simple learning tasks were invested with the growing glamour and prestige of the experimental sciences, and thus made possible the investigation of general learning variables under rigorously controlled conditions.

Thus the more scientifically conducted research in learning theory has been undertaken largely by psychologists unconnected with the educational enterprise who have investigated problems quite remote from the type of learning that goes on in the classroom. The focus has been on animal learning and on short-term and fragmentary rote or nonverbal forms of human learning, rather than on the learning and retention of organized bodies of meaningful material. Experimental psychologists, of course, can hardly be criticized if laboratory studies on nonverbal and rote verbal learning have had little applicability to the classroom. Like all pure research efforts in the basic sciences, these studies were designed to yield only general scientific laws as ends in themselves. The blame, if any is to be assigned, must certainly fall upon educational psychologists who, in general, have failed to conduct the necessary applied research and have succumbed to the temptation of applying the theories and findings of their experimental colleagues to problems of classroom learning.

Finally, for the past thirty years, educational psychologists have been preoccupied with measurement and evaluation, personality development, mental hygiene, group dynamics, and counseling. Despite the self-evident centrality of classroom learning and the cognitive development of the psychological aspects of education, these areas were ignored (Ausubel, 1963) both theoretically and empirically.

Although the withdrawal of educational psychologists from problems of meaningful classroom learning was temporarily expedient, it was, in the long run, very unfortunate on both theoretical and research grounds. In the first place, materials for rote learning are represented and organized quite differently from those for meaningful learning. Not only are the respective learning processess very dissimilar, but the significant variables involved in the two processes are also markedly different, and, where similar, have very different effects. In the second place, it is evident that a distinction must be made between learning tasks involving the short-term acquisition (of single, somewhat contrived concepts, of solution to artificial problems, or of arbitrary associations) in a laboratory setting and the long-term acquisition and retention (of the complex network of interrelated ideas characterizing an organized body of knowledge that is presented to the learner for active incorporation into his cognitive structure) required in a classroom.

Hence the extrapolation of school learning problems from rote learning theory has had many disastrous consequences. It has perpetrated erroneous conceptions about the nature and conditions of classroom learning; it has led educational psychologists to neglect research on factors influencing meaningful learning, hence delaying the discovery of more effective techniques of verbal exposition; and, finally, it has caused some educators to question the relevance of learning theory to the educational enterprise and to formulate theories of teaching that attempt to conceptualize the nature, purposes, and effects of instruction without considering its relationship to learning.

Still another reason for the decline in classroom learning theory can be found in an examination of its historical development during the twentieth century. First, E. L. Thorndike initiated a movement that separated school learning theory from its concern with the acquisition of large bodies of organized knowledge (as represented by the scholastic and humanistic philosophers and by such educational theorists as Herbart) and focused attention on a mechanistic and reductionistic concern with the acquisition of discrete units of such knowledge by rote. This mechanistic concern was reinforced later by behaviorism, neobehaviorism, Pavlovian psychology, a revival of associationism, the functionalism of the twenties and thirties, and Skinnerian psychology and the teaching-machine movement it spawned. Second, the immediate theoretical reaction to connectionism, associationism, and behaviorism, namely the Gestalt and field theory approaches, failed to provide a viable theoretical alternative for educational psychology. Their doctrinaire overemphasis on a perceptual model of learning and retention led to a vastly oversimplified interpretation of the actual learning task involved in the acquisition of subject matter; an overvaluation of the role of stimulus properties and stimulus organization, with a corresponding undervaluation of the role of existing cognitive structure in school learning; an emphasis on nativistic explanatory principles that was quite alien to the very spirit of education; and an unrealistic preoccupation with discovery learning and problem-solving that diverted attention from the more basic reception aspects of classroom learning. Third, John Dewey and the progressive education movement derogated expository teaching, verbal learning, structured learning experience, and the importance of practice and testing, and overemphasized direct, nonverbal, concrete-empirical experience, and learning by discovery.

Prerequisites for a discipline of educational psychology

The foregoing historical considerations and substantive propositions regarding the definition of educational psychology, its relationships to general psychology, and its status as an applied discipline lead to the conclusion that a minimum number of crucial prerequisites must first be met before educational psychology can emerge as a viable and flourishing discipline. First, the acquisition of certain basic intellectual skills, the learning and retention of subject-matter knowledge, and the development of problem-solving capabilities must be regarded as the main practical concerns of theory and research in educational psychology. Second, the attainment of these objectives must be conceptualized as products of meaningful verbal or symbolical learning and retention, and a cogent theory of such learning and retention must be formulated in terms of manipulable independent variables. Third, the elaboration of this theory implies the delineation of unambiguous distinctions between meaningful learning and other forms of learning such as classical and operant conditioning, rote verbal, instrumental, perceptual-motor, and simple discrimination learning. It also implies distinction between varieties of meaningful verbal learning such as representational or vocabulary learning, concept learning, and propositional learning, and between reception and discovery learning. Fourth, meaningful verbal learning must be studied in the form in which it actually occurs in classrooms. In other words, it must be studied as the guided, long-term learning in a social context of large bodies of logically organized and interrelated concepts, facts, and principles rather than as the short-term and fragmented learning of discrete and granulated items of information represented by short-frame teaching-machine programs.

The predicted new look in educational psychology

It is obviously difficult to separate the objective delineation of future research trends in educational psychology from a statement of personal values and preferences in this area. Nevertheless, although frankly acknowledging this serious limitation at the very outset, I still venture to predict the emergence of four major trends in the coming decade. First, I am confident that educational psychologists will return to the classroom to study the kinds of learning processes that are involved in the meaningful acquisition of subject matter, instead of continuing to apply to such processes theories and evidence derived from highly simplified instances of nonverbal or rote verbal learning in laboratory situations. Second, I think we will shortly cease pretending that meaningful classroom learning consists merely of a designated series of problem-solving tasks, and will also make a serious attempt to study the learning of ideas and information presented by teachers and textual materials. Third, I feel reasonably certain that we will devise appropriate methods of investigating the effects of general variables influencing meaningful learning, both singly and in combination, instead of vainly speculating on these effects from the results of particular curriculum improvement projects (e.g., the PSSC and the UICSM) in which an indeterminate number of variables are manipulated in an uncontrolled and indeterminate fashion. Fourth, I am hopeful that we will focus our attention increasingly on the long-term learning and retention of large bodies of sequentially organized subject matter rather than on the short-term mastery of fragmentary learning tasks.

What about the product of this research activity; that is, the future shape of the discipline? I am hopeful that the educational psychology of tomorrow will be primarily concerned with the nature, conditions, outcomes, and evaluation of classroom learning, and will cease to be an unstable and eclectic amalgam of rote learning theory, developmental and social psychology, the psychology of adjustment, mental hygiene, measurement, and client-centered counseling. Thus, hopefully, the new discipline will not consider such topics as child development, adolescent psychology, the psychology of adjustment, mental hygiene, personality, and group dynamics as ends in themselves but will consider them only as they bear on classroom learning. It will confine itself only to psychological theories, evidence, problems, and issues that are of *direct* concern either to the serious student of education or to the future teacher in his role as facilitator of school learning. It will also eliminate *entirely* many topics normally covered in educational psychology courses: the nature and development of needs, general determinants of behavior, general reactions to

frustration, developmental tasks, mechanisms of adjustment, parent-child relationships, noncognitive development during infancy and the preschool years,
and physical development. While it is true that physical development during
childhood affects motor coordination, writing, and popularity in the peer group,
and that physical changes in adolescence affect the self-concept, emotional
stability, peer relations, and athletic skills, an educational psychology course
cannot cover everything. Prospective elementary school teachers will presumably have a course in child development, and prospective secondary school
teachers will presumably have a course in adolescent psychology. Certain
aspects of motivation *are* obviously relevant for classroom learning, but a
general discussion of needs, their nature, function, development, and classification, such as would be appropriate in a course in general psychology, hardly
seems necessary.

One might reasonably anticipate that the new discipline of educational psychology will be concerned principally with meaningful symbolic learning, that
is, reception and discovery that take place in the classroom. Some kinds of
learning, such as rote learning and motor learning are so inconsequential in this
context as to warrant no systematic treatment in a course on educational psychology. Other kinds of learning, for example, the learning of values and attitudes, are not indigenous to the primary or distinctive function of the school
and should be considered only insofar as they affect or are part of the learning
of subject matter. Their more general aspects may be left to such courses as
general and social psychology. And still other kinds of learning: animal learning, conditioning, instrumental learning, and simple discrimination learning are
completely irrelevant to most learning tasks in school, despite the fact that
wildly extrapolated findings in these areas commonly pad many of the educational psychology textbooks. The new discipline, also, will hopefully not be
eclectic in theoretical orientation, but will proceed from a consistent theoretical
framework based on a cognitive theory of meaningful verbal learning. Greater
stress would be placed on cognitive development and the content would be
integrated more closely with related aspects of cognitive functioning.

Finally, an effort should be made to avoid oversimplified explanations,
language, and presentation of ideas, and to employ a level of discourse appropriate to the teaching of educational psychology to prospective teachers and
mature students of education. Educational psychology is a complex rather than a
simple subject. Hence to oversimplify it is to render the beginning student a
serious disservice. Clarity and incisiveness of presentation do not require rever-
sion to a kindergarten level of writing and illustration. In fact, it is the writer's
firm conviction that the thinly disguised contempt many prospective teachers
exhibit for courses in pedagogy and educational psychology stems from the
indefensible attempt to expose them to watered-down, repetitive content and
to an unnecessarily elementary level of vocabulary, sentence structure, illustration, and pedagogic device.

It is true, of course, that if educational psychologists limit their coverage of learning to meaningful verbal learning, the paucity of experimental evidence in this area becomes painfully evident. This paucity is a reflection of the tendency that has prevailed in the past three or more decades for educational psychologists to extrapolate findings from animal, rote, and perceptual-motor learning experiments rather than to do research on meaningful verbal learning. In my opinion, presenting certain significant theoretical propositions to students without definitive empirical support would for the time being be preferable to leaving large gaps in theory or filling them by means of unwarranted extrapolation.

Organization of the discipline

How will the subject matter of the new discipline of educational psychology be organized? Inasmuch as classroom instruction involves the manipulation of those variables influencing learning, a rational classification of learning variables can be of considerable value in clarifying both the nature of the learning process and the conditions that affect it. Such a classification also provides an organizational framework for the field, in a sense, since any course in educational psychology must, of necessity, be organized largely around the different factors influencing classroom learning.

One obvious way of classifying learning variables is to divide them into two categories: intrapersonal (factors within the learner) and situational (factors in the learning situation). The intrapersonal category includes:

(*a*) *cognitive structure variables* — substantive and organizational properties of previously acquired knowledge in a particular subject-matter field that are relevant for the assimilation of another learning task in the same field. Since subject-matter knowledge tends to be organized in sequential and hierarchical fashion, what one already knows in a given field, and how well one knows it, obviously influence one's readiness for related new learnings.

(*b*) *developmental readiness* — the particular kind of readiness that reflects the learner's stage of intellectual development and the intellectual capacities and modes of intellectual functioning characteristic of that stage. The cognitive equipment of the fifteen-year-old learner evidently makes him ready for different kinds of learning tasks than does that of the six- or ten-year-old learner.

(*c*) *intellectual ability* — the relative degree of the individual's general scholastic aptitude (general intelligence or brightness level), and his relative standing with respect to particular differentiated or specialized cognitive abilities. How well a pupil learns subject matter in science, mathematics, or literature obviously depends on his general intelligence, his verbal and quantitative abilities, his problem-solving ability, and his cognitive style.

(*d*) *motivational and attitudinal factors* — desire for knowledge, need for achievement and self-enhancement, and ego-involvement (interest) in a particular kind of subject matter. These general variables affect such relevant conditions of learning as alertness, attentiveness, level of effort, persistence, and concentration.

(*e*) *personality factors* — individual differences in level and kind of motivation, in personal adjustment, in other personality characteristics, and in level of anxiety. Subjective factors such as these have profound effects on quantitative and qualitative aspects of the learning process.

The situational category of learning variables includes:

(*a*) *practice* — its frequency, distribution, method, and general conditions (including feedback or knowledge of results);

(*b*) *instructional materials arrangement* — in terms of amount, difficulty, step size, underlying logic, sequence, pacing, and use of instructional aids;

(*c*) *group and social factors* — such as classroom climate, cooperation and competition, social-class stratification, cultural deprivation, and racial segregation;

(*d*) *characteristics of the teacher* — his cognitive abilities, knowledge of subject matter, pedagogic competence, personality, and behavior.

As Gagne (1967) has written, intrapersonal and situational variables:

undoubtedly have interactive effects upon learning . . . . The external variables cannot exert their effects without the presence in the learner of certain states derived from motivation and prior learning and development. Nor can the internal capabilities of themselves generate learning without the stimulation provided by external events. As a problem for research, the learning problem is one of finding the necessary relationships which must obtain among internal and external variables in order for a change in capability to take place. Instruction may be thought of as the institution and arrangement of the *external* conditions of learning in ways which will optimally interact with the internal capabilities of the learner, so as to bring about a change in these capabilities [p. 295].

The above is not the only meaningful and useful way of classifying this set of learning variables. Another scheme would be to group them into cognitive and affective-social categories. The cognitive category would include the relatively objective intellectual factors, whereas the affective-social category would include the subjective and interpersonal determinants of learning. This scheme of categorization may be somewhat more convenient for the researcher, and may be more familiar to the classroom teacher than is the intrapersonal-situational scheme.

References

AUSUBEL, D. P. The nature of educational research. *Educational Theory*, 1953, **3**, 314-320.

AUSUBEL, D. P. *The psychology of meaningful verbal learning: An introduction to school learning.* New York: Grune & Stratton, 1963.

GAGE, N. L. Theories of teaching. In *Theories of learning and instruction.* Sixty-third Yearbook of the National Society for the Study of Education. Part I. Chicago: University of Chicago Press, 1964. Pp. 268-285.

GAGNE, R. M. Instruction and the conditions of learning. In L. Siegel (Ed.), *Instruction: Some contemporary viewpoints.* San Francisco: Chandler, 1967. Pp. 291-313.

HILGARD, E. R. A perspective on the relationship between learning theory and educational practices. In *Theories of learning and instruction.* Sixty-third Yearbook of the National Society for the Study of Education. Part I. Chicago: University of Chicago Press, 1964. Pp. 402-415.

JERSILD, A. T., & BIENSTOCK, S. F. The influence of training on the vocal ability of three-year-old children. *Child Development,* 1931, **2**, 272-291.

JERSILD, A. T., & BIENSTOCK, S. F. Development of rhythm in young children. *Child Development Monographs,* 1935, No. 22.

MANDLER, G. From association to structure. *Psychological Review,* 1962, **69**, 415-427.

MELTON, A. W. The science of learning and the technology of educational methods. *Harvard Educational Review,* 1959, **29**, 96-106.

SHEFFIELD, F. D. Theoretical considerations in the learning of complex sequential tasks from demonstration and practice. In A. A. Lumsdaine (Ed.), *Student response in programmed instruction.* Washington, D.C.: National Academy of Sciences, National Research Council, 1961. Pp. 13-32.

SMITH, B. O. Critical thinking. In *Recent research and developments and their implications for teacher education.* Thirteenth Yearbook of the American Association of Colleges for Teacher Education. Washington, D.C., 1960. Pp. 84-96.

SPENCE, K. W. The relation of learning theory to the technology of education. *Harvard Educational Review,* 1959, **29**, 84-95.

Psychology in the Teacher-Preparation Program[1]

John Herbert and *Donald Williams*

Should prospective teachers have to study psychology? What psychological knowledge does a teacher need? There are likely to be many different answers to these questions. To the apprentice teacher who dislikes mathematics but is required to take a statistically oriented course in educational psychology, for example, the torture he undergoes seems futile, and nothing the instructor says or does will ever influence his teaching. To the instructor, on the other hand, no subject is more relevant to teaching, for he is certain that current research in his field is producing important results that will revolutionize education.

At present almost everyone who wishes to teach in public elementary and secondary schools is required by college faculties as well as by certification laws to take some courses in psychology. Prospective teachers probably constitute by far the largest group of students enrolled in psychology courses. But what psychology, if any, ought to be offered in teacher-preparation programs, and how much? These questions have been raised by educationists, psychologists, and some of the livelier students, and lately they have been explored by a number of college and university departments and by a state-wide psychological foundations study group in Oregon. The difficulty of finding a widely acceptable answer may be gauged by the fact that in 1965 the Committee to Study the Improvement of Teaching Educational Psychology composed of seven distinguished psychologists,[2] appointed by Division Fifteen of the American Psychological Association and which worked with psychologists across the nation, found that "a detailed specification of the content of educational psychology was a task that was neither appropriate nor possible within the limits of this project [p. 4]."

It would be presumptuous to attempt such a task here.[3] In view of the openness and importance of the question, however, it seems appropriate now to state the issues which seem to be emerging and to call for further discussion. This study, then, is an attempt to sample the range of opinion, with emphasis on material which is not readily accessible in published form; to report some

---

1. This paper was prepared as part of a study undertaken at the request of Reed College and partly financed by the United States Office of Education, Department of Health, Education & Welfare.

2. The members of the committee were: R. Stewart Jones (chairman), Gabriel Della-Piana, Philip Jackson, Bert Y. Kersh, Herbert Klausmeier, Aileen Schoeppe, M. C. Wittrock.

3. For a summary of the topics included in educational psychology textbooks, see Derek N. Nunney, Trends in the content of educational psychology, 1948-63. *Journal of Teacher Education*, 1964, **25** (4), 372-377.

solutions which have been proposed; to stimulate more thorough collection of information and opinion; and, finally, to suggest some directions that might usefully be followed in planning psychology courses for teachers.

The range of opinions

First, of course, there is the question of whether psychology has any place at all in teacher education. Some would deny it. Francis Keppel (1962) gives this description of their view:

> The efforts to use scientific methods to study human behavior seem to them ridiculous if not impious. The result, they say, is a ponderous, pseudo-scientific language which takes ten pages to explain the obvious or to dilute the wisdom long ago learned in humanistic studies. They would argue that a few pages of Bacon or Montaigne are worth more than a three-volume psychological treatise. To build an art of teaching on the basis of the "behavioral sciences", they suggest, is to build on sand [p. 91].

The position Keppel described seems usually to be confined to those who are not themselves responsible for the professional preparation of teachers. Even among those directly concerned with teacher education, there are some, including psychologists, who appear to maintain that teachers ought not to be required to take psychology courses. Examination of their positions, however, usually reveals instead that they favor changes in the form and content of offerings to make them more meaningful and useful to teachers. In private conversations at the University of Chicago, Columbia University, Stanford University, and the University of Toronto, psychologists expressed the opinion that psychology courses *as they are currently taught* are useless or even harmful to the work of teachers. One eminent psychologist said that educational psychology courses offered at present are "baroque and arcane."[4] In the words of another educational and clinical psychologist, they are potentially dangerous because "unless the beginning teacher has help in group management problems . . . the focus on the individual child may well be some barrier rather than a help."[5] The doubts of these psychologists (and of other psychologists and teacher educators) were not based on doubts about the potential importance of the behavioral sciences to teachers generally or of educational psychology in particular. All responded with interest to the question and offered suggestions about what could usefully be taught to teachers. Their views will be presented later in this paper.

Among those who do consider psychology to be actually or potentially valuable to teachers are presumably the large number of staff members of advisory bodies who assist in the setting up of certification requirements and those of university and college programs for teachers who require the study of psychology as part of their program. Although at one time there was widespread criticism of these requirements, closer examination has tended to con-

---

4. Matthew Miles, personal communication, April, 1967.
5. Jacob S. Kounin, personal communication, June, 1967.

firm the need to retain them. James B. Conant (1963) was at first skeptical but came to accept the necessity of some work in psychology, at least for elementary school teachers:

. . . I have been convinced, largely by the testimony of students and teachers, that for those who teach children, psychology has much to say that is so valuable as to warrant the label "necessary", at least for elementary teachers. I believe that research will continue that will yield generalizations sufficiently wide as to be called scientific. As an introduction to the point of view of those concerned with the behavior of animals (including man), a general course in psychology would seem essential [p. 136].

Support for the inclusion of psychology in the teacher-training program also recently came from B. F. Skinner (1965), who comments: "Teachers . . . need the kind of help offered by a scientific analysis of behavior. Fortunately such an analysis is now available [p. 80]." Herbert F. LaGrone, Director of Teacher Education and Media for the American Association of Colleges for Teacher Education, also sees psychology as a useful part of the curriculum for teacher trainees. LaGrone (1964) advocates building a new series of five courses: "Analytical Study of Teaching," "Structure and Uses of Knowledge," "Concepts of Human Learning and Development," "Designs for Teaching-Learning," and "Demonstration and Evaluation of Teaching Competencies" [Pp. 16-58]. Each of these has a psychological component. Those who are concerned with the preparation of teachers of a particular discipline in the secondary schools also consider psychology as a necessary part of that preparation. The Commission on English (1965), for example, recommends that ". . . study in pedagogical processes include . . . one course in the psychology of learning [p. 11]."

Questionnaire results

A substantial number of experienced and student teachers seem to agree that psychology has an important place in teacher preparation, though what little specific information is available suggests that there may be very great diversity of opinion about what aspects of psychology and what kinds of instruction in psychology are useful or interesting.

NEA survey

In a recent survey conducted by the National Education Association, about seven out of every ten teachers responding (92.7% of the sample responded) were satisfied with the contribution psychology courses had made to their success in teaching (see tabulation below). Results given in the published report of the survey (Davis, 1967) are restricted to undergraduate preparation and cannot be analyzed to distinguish teachers with particular graduate degrees. However, when the responses of the 547 teachers with Masters degrees or more were compared with those of the 1,632 teachers with Bachelor degrees or less, the percentage of responses was almost identical, suggesting a very similar attitude towards the psychology courses (as in other recent reports — Frey and Ellis, 1966). The survey is repeated and published at five-year intervals, and the figures given below (Davis, 1967, p. 10) confirm earlier findings.

EVALUATION OF TEACHER PREPARATION
BY 2,344 TEACHERS RESPONDING

Question: In terms of actual contribution to your success in teaching, how would you evaluate the amount and quality of your undergraduate teacher-preparation program in the following areas?

	Amount		Quality		
Subject area	Too Little	About Right	Excellent	Satisfactory	No Preparation or Quality Poor
Psychology of Learning & Teaching	22.1%	68.5	15	68	13.2
Human Growth & Development[a]	19.5	72.7	15.9	66.5	13.3

a. Unpublished information, supplied by Dr. Simeon P. Taylor, Assistant Director, Research Division, National Education Association, Washington, D.C.

Surveys at Cornell and Stanford Universities

Information about the views of experienced teachers who have completed five-year programs is difficult to obtain. A number of programs follow up their students, but their graduates are scattered and the rate of response is generally low. Thus, for example, Kenneth R. Stow's study (1960) at Cornell University, in its survey of 105 graduates who earned the M.Ed. degree between 1954 and 1959, received only seventy-six replies. Stanford University has consistently attempted to obtain information about the graduates of its MAT-type program. A carefully designed questionnaire was sent out each year to all graduates of the program, from 1960, when the first group of twenty-five students completed the course, through 1968, when over one hundred students graduated. In spite of considerable effort to ensure returns, only about 40% of the 400 alumni of the program completed the form. Reed has experienced similar difficulties in obtaining responses to a questionnaire which was sent out this summer. However, after some effort, 108 completed questionnaires were secured from the 115 students who graduated from the MAT program over the last five years.

Even when the rate of response is low, however, the results of these surveys are interesting. It seems significant that although Philosophy of Education was by far the most popular course among graduates of Cornell's Master of Education programs (50.5% reported to have liked this course best), Educational Psychology was rated the most important course (82.6% thought it should be mandatory and 71.1% thought the course in Educational Measurement and

Testing should be mandatory, while 66.6% felt that Philosophy of Education should be required). Results of the annual Stanford survey have not been reported, but another study, Report of the Secondary Education Committee 1967, submitted for use by Stanford instructors and staff members, gives some information about the students' reactions to certain activities in the educational psychology course.

In May 1967 a questionnaire was given to intern teachers at the end of their second quarter at Stanford, and all but five of the 125 students responded. Although no direct question was asked about the usefulness of psychology to teachers, there were some questions about specific aspects of the course. The results are too detailed to be reproduced here, but it seems worthwhile to summarize responses to some of the questions.

The following activities are examples of those found useless by more students than found them useful: the writing of a paper on adolescents, formulation of instructional strategies, study of taxonomies, and participation as subjects in educational experiments. Aspects of the course which the majority of students found useful were: the writing of programs; the formulation of behavioral objectives for a unit and a nine- to twelve-week course; the planning of student evaluation; and "microteaching."[6]

Every topic or activity in educational psychology was either found useful or interesting by some group of students at Stanford. Although the majority of students responding recommended that lectures in educational psychology should be limited to a single summer term, most of the students found a substantial portion of the applied part of the work both useful and interesting.

Survey of MAT graduates at Reed College

At Reed, by means of the questionnaire already referred to, we recently surveyed the opinions of our MAT graduates about the contribution they believed psychology courses had made to their teaching. Some background information may be needed to interpret results. Reed MAT students, like those at Cornell and Stanford, are typically very successful liberal arts graduates who have taken few if any undergraduate courses in psychology or education. Before 1962 the Reed program required very little work in psychology — only a brief portion of a course in the Foundations of Public School Teaching. Offerings in psychology were increased, partly because of certification requirements and partly also at the request of the teaching interns. Until 1964 students normally took two courses in psychology.

In the survey following four questions are related to the students' opinions about the value of psychology courses. The results have not yet been fully analyzed, but some of the main trends are clear. Question 13 asked: "Have you found anything you learned in the psychology courses at Reed helpful in

---

6. Such teaching of small groups of students under close supervision is intended to train new teachers in a particular teaching skill, such as the use of silence or the encouraging of student participation in classroom discussions.

your teaching?" Of the students in the program during the two years from 1962-64, only a few more responded favorably than unfavorably, and in the year 1964-65 the negative replies exceeded the positive ones. Taking the three years together, fewer than 50% of the students found the courses helpful. But in 1965-66 the number of students who believed that the courses were useful in their teaching jumped to 85%, and in 1966-67 the figure remained relatively high at 71%. A similar dramatic reversal occurred in the responses to Question 15: "Did you find the courses useful for purposes other than classroom teaching?" During the two years, 1962-64, students on the whole did not find them useful, by a narrow but definite margin. From 1965-1967, however, three to four times as many students found the courses useful for purposes other than classroom teaching. Answers to Question 16 were more consistent: "Did any of the courses contribute to your general education?" Affirmative answers were given by a substantial majority of the students each year, but even here there was a considerable increase over the last three years. Answers to Question 14 also shifted, but in a somewhat different way. During the first three years more students answered affirmatively than negatively to the question: "Have you found any aspects of psychology that were not covered in the psychology courses at Reed that would have been helpful in your teaching?" During the last two years, however, answers were more evenly divided. This suggests that, as the work in psychology became more relevant to teaching, students felt less need for additional areas to be added to the psychology courses.

TABULATION OF RESPONSES TO QUESTIONNAIRE GIVEN TO REED MAT GRADUATES, SUMMER, 1967.

Numbers in parentheses are percentages of total respondents.

Question 13: Have you found anything you learned in the psychology courses at Reed helpful in your teaching? When and how?

Year	No. of graduates	No. of question-naires returned	Yes	No	Non-commital	No response
1962-3	17	17	8 (47%)	5 (29%)	3 (18%)	1 (6%)
1963-4	23	22	9 (41%)	7 (32%)	4 (18%)	2 (9%)
1964-5	21	18	6 (33%)	9 (50%)	2 (11%)	1 (6%)
1965-6	28	27	23 (85%)	4 (15%)	—	—
1966-7	26	24	17 (71%)	5 (21%)	1 (4%)	1 (4%)
Totals	115	108	63 (58%)	30 (28%)	10 (9%)	5 (5%)

Question 14: Have you found any aspects of psychology that were not covered in the psychology courses at Reed that would have been helpful in your teaching?

Year	No. of graduates	No. of question-naires returned	Needed additional psych. courses	Reed courses sufficient	Non-commital	No response
1962-3	17	17	8 (47%)	3 (18%)	4 (24%)	2 (12%)
1963-4	23	22	9 (41%)	2 (9%)	6 (27%)	5 (23%)
1964-5	21	18	12 (67%)	2 (11%)	—	4 (22%)
1965-6	28	27	13 (48%)	11 (41%)	2 (7%)	1 (4%)
1966-7	26	24	8 (33%)	10 (42%)	2 (8%)	4 (17%)
Totals	115	108	50 (46%)	28 (26%)	14 (13%)	16 (15%)

Question 15: Did you find the courses useful for purposes other than classroom teaching, getting a job, or certification? Yes/No. Which courses were useful and how?

Year	No. of graduates	No. of question-naires returned	Yes	No	Non-commital	No response
1962-3	17	17	7 (41%)	8 (47%)	—	2 (12%)
1963-4	23	22	5 (23%)	9 (41%)	2 (9%)	6 (27%)
1964-5	21	18	11 (61%)	4 (22%)	1 (6%)	2 (11%)
1965-6	28	27	22 (81%)	5 (19%)	—	
1966-7	26	24	18 (75%)	4 (17%)	—	2 (8%)
Totals	115	108	63 (58%)	30 (28%)	3 (3%)	12 (11%)

Question 16: Did any of the courses contribute to your general education? If so, how?

Year	No. of graduates	No. of question-naires returned	Yes	No	Non-commital	No response
1962-3	17	17	9 (53%)	3 (18%)	3 (18%)	2 (12%)
1963-4	23	22	12 (55%)	4 (18%)	1 (5%)	5 (23%)
1964-5	21	18	13 (72%)	2 (11%)	—	3 (17%)
1965-6	28	27	24 (89%)	2 (7%)	—	1 (4%)
1966-7	26	24	20 (83%)	2 (8%)	—	2 (8%)
Totals	115	108	78 (72%)	13 (12%)	4 (4%)	13 (12%)

The results, then, show clearly that while in all years a reasonably large number of students found psychology contributed to their teaching, to other aspects of their work, and to their general education, the feeling was much stronger among students who participated in the program during the last two or three years. Each of the questions called for qualitative answers which have not yet been analyzed but which may throw light on the reasons for the changes in attitude. However, it is possible to speculate without any ready analysis that since the survey (1962-67), there have been no changes in the nature of the student body or in the manner of selecting students, and since changes in staffing were continuous over the whole period, deliberate attempts at changing the courses themselves resulted in changes in the students' reactions. From 1965 on, instructors sought to provide interns with experiences that simulated some important teaching functions and enabled them to use and examine applications of psychology to their own work.[7]

Course content and objectives

Assuming that psychology has a part to play in teacher-preparation programs, the question remains: what should be taught, how, and when? Educational psychologists usually respond to this question by asking for the objectives to be achieved by the teaching. Recently a group of psychologists,[8] after a series of conferences in Oregon, reached the conclusion that courses in psychology in teacher-preparation programs ought to aim at the following outcomes. They should:

(*a*) enable teachers to obtain orderly information about the classroom processes, using the disciplined resources of psychology;

(*b*) enable teachers to take a new look at classroom events, formulate hypotheses about students and learning, and test them to arrive at professional decisions;

(*c*) enable the instructors to screen out from teaching, students incapable of reaching professional decisions;

(*d*) help students to feel positively oriented towards psychological knowledge and skills, so that they will continue to apply them and to learn about them;

(*e*) enable teachers to assume the role of the teacher expected by administrators, parents, and fellow teachers, and to possess the knowledge commonly commanded by professionals;

(*f*) provide the teacher with techniques for handling individual students and groups of students, with ways of shaping their behavior, and with knowledge of how students go about shaping the teacher's behavior;

(*g*) sensitize the teacher to his own students' feelings, for example those of hostility, insecurity, altruism, and helpfulness, and to the ways of considering them in the classroom.

This list of objectives cannot, of course, be taken to represent the views of educational psychologists generally, or even of those who attended the meetings in Oregon, since each item was of primary importance to only some of the

7. A report of this research will be published by Reed College, Portland, Oregon.
8. Psychological Foundations Planning Group, sponsored by the Oregon State Department of Education, Salem, Oregon, under a grant from the U.S. Department of Health, Education and Welfare.

participants. For example, Richard Ripple of Cornell University, who was present as a consultant, considered only the first two objectives to be critical and regarded all the others as definitely secondary. In describing the objectives of the course he teaches at Cornell, Ripple (1967) writes:

> . . . the psychological foundations can be said to be relevant in two general, but distinct ways. First educational psychology, as a body of information, can help in the generation of hypotheses. . . . A second contribution made by educational psychology is that of helping teachers acquire the attitudes and skills necessary to intelligent hypothesizing and the testing of hypotheses. This involves, for example, such skills as how to interpret data intelligently, how to observe accurately, how to avoid fallacies in making unwarranted inferences, how to make adequate decisions regarding what data should be gathered, ways in which data can be gathered and used, etc. [p. 2].

This position is distinctly that of the research-oriented psychologist. It aims at making the teacher a scientist who looks for problems and answers objectively and rigorously.

In contrast, Philip Jackson (1966) starts not from the definition of educational psychology as a field of inquiry, but from the description of the job of the teacher as it really is. "When students are in front of him, and the fat is on the fire," Jackson writes, "the teacher tends to do what he *feels* or *knows* is right rather than with what he *thinks* is right." Of course thought is involved, but ". . . it is thought of quite a different order from that which occurs in an empty classroom [p. 13]."

Psychological theory enters minimally into a teacher's thinking while he is facing his class, according to Jackson,[9] but it can assist him in preparing lessons before the students arrive (for example, considering in advance what to do about Billy who has to go to the toilet all the time) and in evaluating students' performances after they leave the classroom. During these periods, Jackson has said, teaching assumes the appearance of a "highly rational process" in which the teacher uses psychology as one source of information and technique. We need a separate psychology for each of the two kinds of thinking that teachers do.

During the pre-active and post-active periods, according to Jackson, teachers may make decisions and establish and examine hypotheses. What is taught in the usual educational psychology course is relevant here. It is also relevant for another part of the teacher's work, the need to establish himself in the role of teacher and face his public — command the vocabulary of psychology and display the knowledge expected of him. During the period of actual teaching, however, the teacher faces a "social maelstrom" to which the contents of courses and textbooks are irrelevant. He has to hobble along with some advice from the therapists until the social psychologists have more to offer.

Therapists such as Carl Rogers (1964) have still another view of the work of the teacher. His task is to be "a facilitator of significant learning [p. 5]," to

---

9. Philip Jackson, personal communication, April, 1967.

help students (including prospective teachers) learn what they find rewarding and to discover what has meaning in their present experiences. This comes from facing real problems, involving others in problems real to them, accepting with empathy other people's concerns, and becoming sensitive to them. Psychology courses, or better, psychological experiences provided in the teacher-preparation program should not only exemplify these abilities but also help teachers to acquire them.

Social psychologists have something of the same orientation, but with more emphasis on inter-group relationships. Thus Mathew Miles of Teachers College, Columbia University, considers the problem not to be that of providing courses for teachers, but of providing experiences such as sensitivity training, the use of observation techniques, interaction recording systems, and audio and video tapes to obtain information about their own teaching. Further, teachers should be familiar with various ways of shaping behavior and with techniques that produce changes in people's attitudes and conduct. According to Miles,[10] traditional textbooks and courses, for example the sections dealing with learning, are useless in helping teachers to learn to teach or to improve teaching.

Some psychologists, for example Jacob Kounin in the letter cited above, feel even more strongly that help in group management must precede or accompany any work in psychology. Their feeling is supported by the frequency with which student teachers ask for more help in their relationships with their pupils, especially in dealing with discipline problems.

In spite of the great diversity of opinion, psychologists, educationists, administrators, teachers, and student teachers appear to identify the difficulties in a similar way, stressing the need for a more appropriate relationship between the academic study of educational psychology as a field of inquiry and the professional study of psychology in the preparation of classroom teachers.[11] Virtually every psychologist whose views were sought, including some not quoted here, expressed strong faith in the potential efficacy of psychological knowledge and skill to make a contribution to the performance of teachers,[12] but everyone either expressed strong doubts about the adequacy of the standard lecture course as a means to that end or else totally condemned the traditional course offerings.

When Philip Jackson, Jacob Kounin, and Mathew Miles talk about the kind of training that would be helpful to teachers, they have in mind a series of experiences which would enable teachers to understand better how and why people, primarily themselves and students but also parents and administrators, respond to others. They do not mean a series of talks or even demonstrations or discussions, but a set of carefully planned activities involving the student teacher

10. Mathew Miles, personal communication, April, 1967.

11. For a similar position in the United Kingdom, see Committee on Higher Education, *Evidence*, Part I, Vol. A, p. 107. Published with *Higher education: Report of the committee appointed by the Prime Minister under the chairmanship of Lord Robbins, 1961-63*. London: Her Majesty's Stationery Office, 1963.

12. This is a change from the past. See, for example, James, Symonds, Watson, etc.

directly in the use and evaluation of psychological knowledge. Ripple also recognizes the need for classroom applications, though he would prefer to consider this the field of the colleague responsible for teaching methods while the professor of educational psychology teaches teachers to invent and test psychological hypotheses.

Frederick J. McDonald of Stanford University, on the other hand, would welcome the opportunity to teach the applications as well as the theory of particular units of psychology, partly because of the greater psychological efficacy of this combination and partly because of the opportunity to obtain feedback from students for research purposes.[13]

We do not have the data to make inferences about the kind of work in psychology that Conant, the Commission on English, the students at Cornell, or the teachers surveyed by the NEA would like to have offered to teachers. We do know, however, that LaGrone, the fifth-year students at Stanford, and the teachers who had received the Reed MAT degree responded favorably to those parts of the program which bore most directly on teaching.

Recognizing then the need to teach the classroom applications of psychological theory in new ways, one must also recognize a serious obstacle in the way of improvement. Teaching by providing experiences, whether they are of group interaction, of classroom events, of evaluative techniques, or of shaping student behavior or other aspects of psychology, is very demanding of staff and time. It certainly cannot be done satisfactorily in a course which at the same time attempts to give an organized survey of the total field of educational psychology, the sources of knowledge, and the techniques of research.

Possible solutions

One solution might be to select only the most useful aspects of educational psychology and teach them theoretically and practically. Thus one might select testing and measurement or developmental psychology or learning or group interaction, depending on the preferences of the department or the instructor. This selective emphasis, however, would leave untouched most of the potential contributions of psychology to teaching and so leave the student in ignorance of many resources.

Another possible solution is the one which was proposed but eventually rejected at the State University of New York at Stony Brook (Peters, 1965). Each student was to have the right to choose one behavioral science (for example, anthropology, sociology, or psychology) for study in depth, taking several courses in the particular field, in the expectation that this would enable him to bring the resources of that discipline to bear on his teaching and the examination of his teaching in an organized manner. One may well wonder whether the ability to make independent pedagogical applications would necessarily result from the academic study of any discipline. One may also maintain

---

13. Frederick J. McDonald, personal communication, July, 1967.

that psychology has a contribution to make to teaching and that no prospective teacher should be deprived of it.

A third suggestion made in conversation by McDonald would substitute for the lecture course given by one instructor, a course in which a number of instructors would first lecture on their own specialties and then work through the applications of the topic discussed, using classroom experiences and research as needed.[14] Though this might be an ideal solution, it is administratively difficult to achieve. Even a university of the distinction of Stanford might have difficulty in coordinating and staffing a course of this type. Other institutions, especially smaller ones, are not likely to have enough staff members both expert in an area of psychology and knowledgeable about classroom teaching.

Programs for teacher education may well want to experiment with a dual approach, offering two-function-oriented courses instead of the traditional subject-oriented courses called Testing & Measurement, Child Development, Guidance, and such. One would be a theoretical course, aimed at achieving the first four objectives identified by the Oregon Committee: the ordering of data, the use of the discipline of psychology, the formulation of hypotheses, and the screening out of students incapable of making professional judgments. This course would also seek to enable teachers to assume the role of the professional educator, versed in the language of psychology.

This course then could form the foundation of an analytic-applied course, aimed at the other three objectives of the Oregon Committee: to help teachers feel that psychology is helpful to them in their contact with students and in classroom decisions, to sensitize the teacher to his own and his students' feelings, and (together with the methods courses and the practical experience) to provide the insight necessary to incorporate the daily teaching experience into an intellectually integrated whole.

The theoretical course might well resemble some parts of currently offered courses, using materials, tests, and ideas such as those which are described in the *Handbook for Instructors of Educational Psychology* or some of the more recent textbooks. Laboratory tasks would be related to this course, as they are now in many of the more effective programs. Students, aware that direct classroom applications would be developed in the applied-analytic course, could use their academic skills without the defensive reaction which comes when professional preparation is expected within an academic teaching format.

A. W. Foshay, of Teachers College, Columbia University, forsees a possible further development:

We could think in terms of satellite courses, around a core psychology course. The core course would be taught by a psychologist and would contain psychological theories, research, etc. The satellite courses would be designed to help teachers apply the materials, and would be taught by professionals who were specially capable in assisting teachers to apply the psychological knowledge to their work.

The intention then would be to prepare teachers who practiced the profession of

---

14. Frederick J. McDonald, private communication, July, 1967.

pedagogy. They would be trained, partly through practice, to see the reasons behind the way teachers teach, even when the experienced teachers themselves do not know. They would cease to see teaching as a bag of tricks. When experienced teachers suggest to them that it is important to start lessons definitely, they would be aware of the psychological reasons.[15]

Development needed

At present there are substantial difficulties facing the establishment of such a cluster of courses. One is the problem of working out the exact relationship between theoretical and applied courses, and in particular, the relationship of the instructors to one another and to the students. Perhaps progress along those lines is more likely to occur in the smaller colleges where classes are smaller, the possibility of experimenting with different course structures and faculty relationships is greater, and the problem of providing laboratory experiences in the schools is less overwhelming.

An equally serious problem is the scarcity of generally available materials for the applied work. Unlike the instructors of the theoretical, experimental or educational psychology courses, the faculty member attempting an analytic-applied course has to improvise his own movies, tapes, cases, and even tests; a time-consuming, wasteful, and unreliable process. There is a great need for help for teachers of applied courses. The answer to this need potentially could come from a sharing of resources among colleges, school districts, and research institutes, to develop viable applied-analytic courses for instructors to adopt and adapt. However, leadership could hardly be expected from school districts or small colleges, which are unlikely to have the resources. It is ultimately the responsibility of large universities and research institutes. Courses need to be planned, outlined and developed; materials created, tried out, and evaluated — so that professors of psychology and curriculum departments could work with teacher educators in an effective formulation of a program to help teachers in their increasingly complex work.

References

AUSUBEL, D. P. *Educational psychology: A cognitive view*. New York: Holt, Rinehart and Winston, 1968.

BIGGE, M. L., & HUNT, M. P. *Psychological foundations of education: An introduction to human development and learning*. New York: Harper and Row, 1962.

BLAIR, G. M., JONES, R. S., & SIMPSON, R. S. *Educational psychology*. (2nd ed.) New York: Macmillan, 1962.

CARPENTER, F., & HADDAN, E. *Systematic applications of psychology to education*. New York: Macmillan, 1964.

COMMISSION ON ENGLISH. *Freedom and discipline in English*. New York: College Entrance Examination Board, 1965.

COMMITTEE ON HIGHER EDUCATION. *Higher education: Report of the committee appointed by the Prime Minister under the chairmanship of Lord Robbins, 1961-63*. 7 vols. London: Her Majesty's Stationery Office, 1963.

15. Arthur W. Foshay, private communication, April, 1967.

COMMITTEE TO STUDY THE IMPROVEMENT OF TEACHING EDUCATIONAL PSYCHOLOGY. R. Steward Jones, chairman. *Handbook for instructors of educational psychology.* Urbana: University of Illinois, 1965.

CONANT, J. B. *The education of American teachers.* New York: McGraw-Hill, 1963.

CRONBACH, L. J. in consultation with Hilgard, E., and Spalding, W. *Educational psychology.* (2nd ed.) New York: Harcourt, Brace and World, 1963.

CROW, L. D., & CROW, A. *Educational psychology.* (Rev. ed.) New York: American Book Company, 1963.

DAVIS, H. Professional preparation for teaching. In *The American public school teacher, 1965-1966.* Research Report 1967-R4. Washington, D.C.: National Education Association of the United States, 1967.

DOLL, R. C. *Curriculum improvement: Decision-making and process.* Boston: Allyn and Bacon, 1964.

FRANDSEN, A. N. *Educational psychology: The principle of learning in teaching.* New York: McGraw-Hill, 1961.

FREY, S., & ELLIS, J. Educational psychology and teaching: Opinions of experienced teachers. *The Teachers College Journal,* 1966, **38** (3), 88-91.

INTERN ADVISORY COMMITTEE, School of Education, Stanford University. Report to the secondary education committee, Stanford, May 22, 1967. (Dittoed.)

JACKSON, P. The way teaching is. In Curtice Hitchcock (Ed.), *The way teaching is.* Seminar on Teaching, Washington, D.C., 1965. Association for Supervision and Curriculum Development and the Center for the Study of Instruction of the National Education Association, 1966.

JAMES, W. *Talks to teachers on psychology and to students on some of life's ideals.* New York: H. Holt and Company, 1914.

KEPPEL, F. The education of teachers. In H. Chauncey (Ed.), *Talks on American education.* New York: Teachers College Press, Teachers College, Columbia University, 1962. Pp. 83-94.

KLAUSMEIER, H. J., & Goodwin, W. *Learning and human abilities: Educational psychology.* (2nd ed.) New York: Harper and Row, 1966.

KOLESNIK, W. B. *Educational psychology.* New York: McGraw-Hill, 1963.

LAGRONE, H. F. *A proposal for the revision of the pre-service professional component of a program of teacher education.* Washington, D.C.: American Association of Colleges for Teacher Education, 1964.

LINDGREN, H. C. *Educational psychology in the classroom.* (3rd ed.) New York: John Wiley and Sons, 1967.

McDONALD, F. J. *Educational psychology.* (2nd ed.) Belmont, California: Wadsworth Publishing Company, 1965.

MORSE, W. C., & WINGO, G. M. *Psychology and teaching.* (Rev. ed.) Chicago: Scott, Foresman and Co., 1962.

MOULY, G. J. *Psychology for effective teaching.* New York: Holt, Rinehart and Winston, 1960.

NUNNEY, D. N. Trends in the content of educational psychology, 1948-63. *Journal of Teacher Education,* 1964, **15** (4), 372-377.

OLSON, W. C. *Psychological foundations of the curriculum* (UNESCO), 1957, **26**, 5-67.

PETERS, F. R. Considerations leading to a new program in education for students who plan to teach. State University of New York at Stony Brook, December, 1965. (Mimeographed.)

PRESSEY, S. L., ROBINSON, F. P., & HORROCKS, J. E. *Psychology in education.* New York: Harper and Row, 1959.

RIPPLE, R. E.   Education 511: Educational psychology. Ithaca, N.Y.: Cornell University, 1967. (Mimeographed.)

ROGERS, C.   What psychology has to offer teacher education. Paper prepared for the Conference on Educational Foundations, Cornell University, April 27-28, 1964. (Mimeographed.)

ROGERS, C.   *Five fields and teacher education.* Ithaca, N.Y.: Cornell University Project One Publication, 1965.

SHOBEN, E. J.   Psychology in the training of teachers. *Teachers College Record,* 1964, **65**, 436-440.

SKINNER, B. F.   Why teachers fail. *Saturday Review,* **48** (October 16, 1965), 80-1, 98-102.

SKINNER, B. F.   *The technology of teaching.* New York: Appleton-Century-Crofts, 1968.

STEPHENS, J. M.   *Educational psychology: The study of educational growth.* (Rev. ed.) New York: Holt, Rinehart and Winston, 1956.

STEPHENS, J. M.   *The psychology of classroom learning.* New York: Holt, Rinehart and Winston, 1965.

STOW, K. R.   A study of the master of education programs at Cornell University. Unpublished Masters thesis, Cornell University, 1960. (Typewritten.)

SYMONDS, P. M.   *What education has to learn from psychology.* New York: Teachers College Press, Teachers College, Columbia University, 1960.

THOMPSON, G. G., GARDNER, E. F., & DiVESTA, F.   *Educational psychology.* New York: Appleton-Century-Crofts, 1959.

THYNE, J. M.   *The psychology of learning and techniques of teaching.* London: University of London Press, 1963.

TROW, W. C.   *Psychology in teaching and learning.* L. Carmichael (Ed.), Boston: Houghton Mifflin Co., 1960.

WATSON, G.   *What psychology can we trust?* New York: Teachers College Press, Teachers College, Columbia University, 1961.

ISSUES AND POSITIONS

A None-too-friendly Look at the Contribution of Educational Psychology to Teacher Training[1]

Floyd G. Robinson

In the limited scope of this paper the following questions will be examined:

(*a*) What is the intent of educational psychology?

(*b*) To what extent is this intent realized in current textbooks?

(*c*) What might be done to improve the content of educational psychology?

(*d*) What experiences should be planned for the teacher in training which go beyond subjecting him to improved content?

Before turning to these major questions, there are some preliminary issues that should be discussed. It must be acknowledged that the problem of introducing an appropriate course of educational psychology into teacher training is part of a much larger task of bringing psychological knowledge to bear upon educational decision-making in general. I believe that two unfortunate consequences will follow any attempt to treat the problem of teacher training in isolation. The lesser evil is that we tend to pad our courses with information which the classroom teacher cannot use, because the proposed action lies mostly outside his domain of decision-making. For example, theories of cognitive development might have something to say about a child when he is ready to learn particular concepts, and thus about how curriculum content should be spaced out over the grade structure; but the decision as to which concepts should be taught at which grade level is made largely by the curriculum developer rather than by the teacher. Similarly, while educational psychology has many useful things to say about practice, the existing freedom for constructing practice schedules are pretty well taken up by the author of the reading text, the arithmetic text, or spelling text. It might be interesting to speculate upon the extent to which such devices as programmed instruction, educational television, and explicit teaching procedures derived from task analysis either eliminate independent teacher behavior altogether or enmesh him so tightly in

---

1. This paper has also been published in *Readings in school learning,* edited by David Ausubel. New York: Holt, Rinehart & Winston, 1969.

specific procedural directions that the teacher's knowledge of educational psychology could hardly be a significant variable affecting student learning.

Another consequence of treating teacher education in isolation is that we easily forget that the failure of both psychology and educational psychology to make an impact at those levels of decision-making where the real character and substance of public education is decided will mean that our intervention in teacher education may have only a secondary or peripheral effect. Indeed, I will conclude my paper by arguing that unless some substantial changes are made in the expectations which exist at these higher decision-making levels, inventive methodology devised with the aid of educational psychology is almost certain to be defeated.

Some documentation of our failure to influence high-level decision-making could be found in the field of mathematics education. More than a decade ago when the first wave of the mathematics revolution rocked our traditional viewpoint, it was hoped that an opportunity had arisen to introduce psychological insights into educational practice via the new curricula. Many efforts were made to bring psychologists and mathematicians together to achieve that end. The results, however, were disastrous as far as psychology was concerned, for mathematicians rapidly concluded that psychologists had little to tell them. In my opinion the current attitude of mathematicians and mathematics methodologists toward the potential contribution of educational psychology is best epitomized by the prestigious Cambridge Report on *Goals for School Mathematics* (1963), which ticked off Piaget with the simple assertion that his theoretical and experimental work had no relevance for the major reform of mathematics education proposed by them.

Mathematicians, then, have proceeded to take matters into their own hands, have completely dominated the thinking that lies behind new programs in secondary school mathematics, and in many cases, are even exercising critical influence on the programs designed for *elementary school* children. In pontificating on the appropriateness of different levels of abstraction at different ages, on the proper sequencing of ideas, and on appropriate methods of presentation, the mathematicians have become the *de facto* educational psychologists in mathematics. Moreover, since mathematicians and other university subject-matter specialists definitely have the upper hand in instituting curriculum reform and influencing the educational hierarchy, their active disdain for the educational psychologist is likely to have important implications for teacher training. For example, while many of the proposed reforms of educational psychology try to increase the offerings in teacher-training programs, by increasing the length of teacher-training programs, the additional time made available will however be used by subject-matter specialists, who are determined that teachers in training should receive more instruction in their substantive fields. As an example of the trend of local events I would point out that in Ontario, a province blessed by both strong psychology and educational psychology communities, we have recently established a Master of Arts in Teaching degree in mathematics, the precursor of general developments in this field.[2] In the midst of expanding educational psychology it is interesting to note that the typical course pattern for the MAT is four courses in graduate level mathematics and one course in educational theory, and that the latter need not be educational psychology nor any of its near relatives (measurement, curriculum development, research, etc.). It is clear then that the prestigious educators of mathematics education look upon the master teacher as a person who has no need for the insights of educational psychology. The major implication to be drawn from the preceding observations is that any plan for the reform of educational psychology in teacher education must take into account the existing power structure in educational decision-making. This question will be dealt with later in this paper.

The intent of educational psychology programs in teacher-training institutions

What is the purpose of educational psychology? Judging from the textbooks and the writings of those who express themselves coherently on the subject, I believe that the intention is to create a kind of input-output model. According to this conception, the "output" would be a class of variables comprising those outcomes that are considered to be the school's responsibility. The "inputs" represent a class of psychological variables or variables linked to mediating psychological variables, known to be causally linked to the desired behavioral outcomes, the manipulation or accommodation of which lies within the school's power. Such an input-output conception is clearly visible in our writing efforts. We explicitly categorize behavioral outcomes in such terms as concept learning, generalization learning, problem-solving, creativity, and the like. Moreover the bulk of our text is concerned with empirical evidence and logical argument linking a great variety of cognitive, affective, social, situational, and task variables to these outcomes. And to varying degrees, different authors attempt to formulate a set of unifying ideas which allow some economy in predicting, explaining, or simply organizing the vast multitude of potential relationships.

When we intervene in teacher training, we assume that the teacher will be able to superimpose this input-output mesh upon his classroom decision making, and that, as a result, decisions will be reached which, as the common wording goes, "will optimize or maximize the product." I think it unfortunate that this rather facile assumption has never been scrutinized by detailed analysis. It seems that we must possess an infinite amount of uncertainty as to what the optimum program might be or even what the optimum individual choice will be in a particular situation, and that the application of any empirically derived generalization (which is capable of reducing uncertainty by a finite amount) will still leave us mightily uncertain. In this respect, the only conclusion I can come to is that we had best cease speaking of the maximum or optimum when referring to procedures that might be concocted for classroom use on the basis of educational psychology. More realistically, one could probably demon-

---

2. MA(T) degree offered by the University of Toronto.

strate that the assignment of the values of input variables based on empirically derived generalization would produce a probability of increasing the value of some well-defined output function over that of the values normally assigned by a teacher whose intuitive generalizations disagreed with empirically derived ones.

I am, then, prepared to believe on purely logical grounds that educational psychology *can* have some positive influence on decision-making. But I cannot accept the facetious platitudes on the benefits to be derived from our field, which are advanced largely by questionable analogy and by our spokesmen and textbook writers. But even my more modest formulation of benefits to be conferred requires that the essence of our discipline, the propositions or generalizations which we formulate, must meet the following requirements:

(*a*) The generalization has to be incorporable into the cognitive structure which is activated by the teacher while operating in the classroom. The concepts and variables of the generalization contained in it must have meaning for the teacher to the extent where their values or exemplars can be unequivocally identified.

(*b*) The generalization has to suggest manipulations of input variables or methods of accommodating input variables over which the teacher has some control.

(*c*) The generalization has to suggest manipulations which the teacher would not ordinarily arrive at by simple inspection of the situation or by more profound intuition.

(*d*) The generalization has to be valid, that is, to reduce uncertainty in an objective sense.

The generalizations meeting these criteria would be referred to as simply "potentially useful" generalizations in the rest of the paper.

The educational psychology literature

Given that our intent is to create an input-output system, we must next ask to what extent this intent is realized in our current textbooks. The deficiencies I will cite are those I first discovered in my own recent attempts to write a textbook on educational psychology.

Undoubtedly part of our difficulty in formulating useful generalizations in educational psychology can be traced to the fact that while we borrow many of our concepts from academic psychology, we show a curious tendency to avoid approaching that discipline. On the one hand, we are attracted by its power to confer respectability upon our work; on the other hand, we are anxious to take our audience into account. The typical compromise reached in dealing with the concepts of psychology is to water down their definitions in language thought to be more congenial to the teacher's ear. The result is that even the most rigorously defined concepts acquire a gratuitous aura of ambiguity in the translation. For example, the common definition of a positive reinforcer as "a stimulus whose presentation strengthens the response which it follows" remains ambiguous because the word "strengthens" is undefined and is exceedingly misleading. Not many would attempt to improve on this definition by defining "strengthen" in terms of the probability of a response and by indicating how this probability is to be measured. If we begin so far from the accurate definition of a concept which is capable of clarity, it is understandable that as we engage intrinsically vaguer terms like "motivation," "personality," "need," "problem," or "ability," the informality of our language increases to the point where it is difficult to see how the student can emerge with a clear concept. Such beginnings augur an unfortunate ending; for from fuzzy concepts one can generate only chaotic generalizations.

The substance of the generalization itself introduces another problem. I think the typical approach of the educational psychology textbook writer might be described as an eclectic-translative one, in that he grasps hold of the established psychological theory or hypotheses resulting from laboratory studies, and uses these as the bases of hypotheses or inferences to what will happen in what he regards as an analogous educational situation. No doubt this approach will keep educational psychology *au courant* with the advance of psychological knowledge in general and has the further advantages that it is both interesting and comfortable for the writer and lecturer. For example, it is attractive to many minimally qualified instructors because a one-lecture-stand on Berlyne's theory of transformational thinking or on operant conditioning, in addition to generating interest, does not allow time for perceptive students to collect their thoughts sufficiently to ask embarrassing questions.

The eclectic-translative approach, however, suffers from sizeable weaknesses. The most dangerous one is that at least some of the extrapolations appear to be *invalid* because the assumed analogous situations in the classroom are simply not analogous. We all *say* that the phenomena of the classroom are of a different order of complexity from those of the psychological laboratory and that one cannot indiscriminately extrapolate from the simple to the complex. Yet our conviction does not necessarily go with this assertion. For we seem to persist in citing the interference theory of forgetting, with its implications of the inevitability of retroactive inhibition, the operant conditioning view that explicit reinforcements ought to be built into instructional materials, or the Thorndike-Skinner view that aversive stimulation is generally ineffective and should be avoided as a classroom motivational device. Yet the tenability of such generalizations, when examined in terms of the actual complexity of the learning of an organized body of knowledge and the sophisticated motivations in the school setting, seem highly questionable and can hardly be thought to have a positive influence on classroom decision-making.

Another tendency inherent in the loose structure of an eclectic approach is that of backing ourselves into elaborate tautologies. Many writers, for example, during the rapid review of learning theory, define a positive reinforcer as the stimulus that strengthens the response it follows. Fifty pages later, in the discussion of motivation, they can be found advising teachers that if they require a particular behavior to recur they should make sure that an appropriate positive reinforcement follows the desired response. Putting these statements together, the teacher has now been informed that to make behavior recur he must provide something that will make it more likely to recur. Somehow this does not seem very helpful.

Our writing is not sufficiently sustained to carry us all the way to complex tautology and we stop at mere meaningless generalization. For example, we say that "authoritarian teachers tend to depress pupils' creativity" — leaving both "authoritarian" and "creativity" undefined. These faults of tautology and meaninglessness cannot, of course, be entirely attributed to the eclectic-translative approach. We are in danger whenever we inch toward generalization with little more than syntax as a restraining influence.

Not all our generalizations are fuzzy, however; many are clear enough but stand at a great distance from any suggested or implied action. Such, for example, are detailed data — including graphs and charts — on the relative height and broad-jumping abilities of boys and girls at various ages, on the distribution of socio-economic classes in particular towns, on the improvement of maze learning with practice, or on the forgetting of nonsense syllables over varying periods of time. One might argue that by understanding such relationships the teacher acquires a firmer grasp of the phenomena of education; yet, in the absence of any manipulable variable, I find it difficult to believe that any of these statements would figure prominently in the improvement of educational product.

Of course it would be unfair to assert that *all* educational psychology consists of nothing more than erroneous, tautologous, vague or inconsequential generalizations. In fact, a good part of the writing is merely descriptive and when this is done accurately — as, for example, in elaborating a system of behavioral outcomes or describing a particularly relevant experiment — the product can have some value. Moreover, some of the generalizations offered do seem to me to meet the criteria of potential usefulness cited in an earlier section. And yet I feel that my bland descriptions have not really captured the "unreal" feel of the prose in this field. To do this, one must make two excursions, first by sampling intact sections of writing rather than isolated generalizations, and second by proceeding to those remarkable final statements of advice which conclude the textbook writers' labors.

As to the first excursion, the stringing together of a series of undefined terms and vague generalizations described above reaches its most ludicrous extreme in the numerous five-page summaries of Piaget's theory, the last part of which typically begins in the following fashion: "In the stage of 'formal' operations, beginning somewhere in the 11-15 age group, the child acquires the ability to undertake 'combinatorial,' 'hypothetical deductive' and 'if-then' thinking. At this stage the child is no longer bounded by the 'empirical givens' but can hypothesize and is capable of 'thinking about thinking.' . . ." This account is typically larded with further undefined terms (curiously set in quotation marks as if this practice somehow explained their meaning) and several incomprehensible passages from Piaget himself. Such small snatches as I have been able to understand strike me as being terribly misleading and I find it difficult to believe that the teacher can profit much from them.

Our second excursion is to travel to the back of the chapter where, having now defined concepts and formulated generalizations, the textbook writer must offer the teacher some straightforward advice on how to manipulate input variables. Here, I feel educational psychology sinks to levels of banality unmatched in any other scientific or professional writing. "The teacher," we announce with a straight face, "must keep in mind that her pupils are individuals, each with his own unique pattern of abilities." The teacher should remember that "not all pupils are motivated toward school work," and that "the child should move at the pace determined by his abilities." This is as patronizing and insulting as it would be to inform a neophyte physicist that "objects generally fall downward, other things being equal," or the medical student that "patients are not always as sick as they think they are."

In summary, it seems that educational psychology, as represented by the texts which we put into the hands of teachers in training, moves through the progressive errors of defining its concepts poorly, fashioning generalizations by an uninhibited translation of psychological theory into the educational situation, and abstracting from these generalizations some pitiful caricature of good advice. By the end of these wretched essays I think we know that we have said very little of any real value to the teacher. The impression which experienced teachers take from our writing, if I might cite a response from a course evaluation,[3] is that "after a bold initial sally in which educational psychologists cite the importance of a particular topic, they retreat from the phenomenon as it is found in the classroom with frightening acceleration, resorting in the final stages to covering their tracks with desperately spiralling verbal gymnastics."

Reforming the educational psychology text

I believe it will be worthwhile to reform the educational psychology text because, aside from what may happen in a few advanced experimental programs, what the typical teacher is likely to know about our discipline will be the content of the text, coupled with such folksy elaborations as may be offered by a none-too-well qualified instructor. Such reform will not be an easy task, since the text is oriented toward a large commercial market that seems to impose its own conditions for approval. Surely, it can only be an illusion that the marketplace demands such complete coverage that we have been induced to range so

---

3. Based on a response to a course evaluation questionnaire which was sent out by the Applied Psychology Department of OISE in 1966 to students in the educational psychology course.

widely over the cognitive, affective, and motor domains, adding statistics and evaluation, and providing liberal extractions from learning theory, developmental psychology, and personality theory.

We seem terribly afraid of leaving anything out; yet common sense informs us that coverage must be narrowed if our writing is to acquire any depth, and with less coverage, perhaps we can make some inroads on the problem of vague terminology. No writer can emerge with a universally accepted and for-all-times definition of "problem-solving," but he should be expected to be consistent in the use of this term throughout his tome and to distinguish it from "creativity" or "discovery" if he uses the latter terms.

But a bigger step forward will come when we are able to wean ourselves from the eclectic-translative approach that characterizes contemporary educational psychology. While it can be interesting, its net effect is like shining a number of small colored lights on a vast dark object; there are points of brilliance here and there but the total structure of the object and the relationship of its parts remain invisible. It would be preferable to decide on the categories of behaviors we are interested in producing, in public education, and to stick doggedly to the phenomena defined by these categories as they exist in the classroom. For example, keeping in mind that problem solving is an appropriate educational goal, let us analyze the characteristics of problems as they exist in the context of complex bodies of knowledge taught in school, let us define some reasonable criteria for setting off problems from lower orders of behavioral outcomes, and let us exemplify how strategies can be devised to lead students to independent solution of classes of such problems. By all means let us draw upon laboratory psychology where it is appropriate, but there is an immense difference in the resulting utility between making the classroom phenomena the focal point of our discussion and wandering vaguely through *einstellung* effects, the two pendulum problem, *ex post facto* habit family analyses of problem solving, Dewey's five stages, and a host of other miscellania.

And where, as is usually the case, definitive empirical evidence is lacking, I would not hesitate to speculate on the basis of analysis and deduction from a set of theoretical constructs. Such approaches are, after all, luxuries unavailable to the harried teacher and their application may cast light on classroom learning. Of several instances that might be cited, I would think that much of the impressive success of task analysis in recent years can be attributed to the power of reasoning, unfettered by psychological dogma. Thus Piaget's theory argues that children will not ferret out the cause-effect relationships in natural phenomena until their mental operations form the complex structure characteristic of the formal stage of thinking. But task analysis, abetted by straightforward reasoning, suggests that Piaget has read too much into the problem and that the child can, given a small amount of training, produce acceptable solutions at much younger ages. Although no hard data appears to be available, the task analysis conclusion should be entered as a relevant educational hypothesis and guide to the teacher's action.

Beyond the textbook

One might thus envisage an educational psychology text of the future containing a number of useful generalizations, either empirically derived or speculative, bearing on classroom learning and organized around the central concepts of the nature of the learner and the learning process. I would say that generalizations concerning the efficacy of advance organizers, or the distinctive kinds of stimulus support (dependence upon empirical props) required by children at different stages of cognitive development, or the differential relationship of arousal — manifested by drive level, emotion or anxiety — to performance of simple as opposed to complex tasks, all satisfy my criterion of potential usefulness and can be incorporated into a larger ideational structure.

These are *potentially* useful generalizations but they are not likely to be used by the individual classroom teacher. The difficulty is that these are *indeed* generalizations across tasks, personality types, motivational states and — most important — subject-matter areas. They are not ready for incorporation into the teacher's decision-making structure without further adaptation at least to the level of his particular subject-matter field. One can understand well enough the general principle of organizers, but it takes a good deal of initiative and invention actually to construct an organizer for an algebra passage, or to discern the proper placement, level of generality, and method of incorporation of a series of organizers into an algebra course.

Now while we intimate in our educational psychology textbooks that the teacher ought to do this applied research, we cannot realistically expect this to happen. The teacher will not do it even if he has the time because the teacher's decision-making schema are completely preempted by the ultra-specific procedural rules of the methodologist who, not content to speak of trends, general relationships or suggestions, tells the teacher which book to buy, how to teach specific lessons, how much homework to assign, what to write on the board, what to put on the bulletin board, and so on. Moreover, these specific procedural rules are reinforced by observation, practice teaching, and written examinations. It is not surprising then that they tend to be prepotent from the moment a teacher steps into the class, and that the teacher finds they will work well enough, at least up to whatever ambiguous standard he may be able to fashion, without training in evaluation. Furthermore, the teacher, particularly in his early years, is in a high-anxiety situation, a state that does not lend itself to that more extended reflection that draws upon remote rules, peripheral knowledge. Thus an initial prepotency, energized by a high drive level and lack of opportunity for critical assessment, causes the methodological rules to congeal rapidly into fixed habits, while the airy generalizations of educational psychology travel the way of all unused ideas.

In view of the prevailing power structure in education, and for reasons previously cited, the "enlightened" methodologist will, during the next few years, provide the best hope for educational psychology to make an impact through teacher training (as opposed to contributions at higher levels). It is within

the framework of inventive methodology that the potentially useful generalizations of educational psychology, together with other ingredients, make up the
detailed procedural rules for developing specific kinds of behavior in the school
setting. This is not to say that methodology will ever be a derivative of psychology, for the former is still largely an inventive process and seems likely
to remain so. How educational psychology contributes to the process of
methodological invention will vary from case to case. Sometimes it may suggest
a procedure directly; more often, however, it may merely act as a set of logical
and empirical constraints upon otherwise freewheeling hypothesizing about
procedures.

Perhaps my view of the ultimate relationship between educational psychology
and methodology is too much colored by personal experience. For some years
as a classroom teacher, I labored unsuccessfully to inculcate in my students the
ability to solve the geometry problems to which we were all subjected in our high
school days. Even though I was unsuccessful, I expect I would have gone on for
thirty years with the procedural rules taught in the methodology courses had
I not been diverted by the enticements of graduate study. Anyway, I came back
to the problem many years later and worked out a strategy that seems to allow
much younger children to cope with these logical exercises, even to the point
of handling problems which they have not seen before. When embroiled in the
kind of discussion underlying this conference, I have often reflected on the
contribution of educational psychology to this small personal triumph in
methodological invention. For the most part this success was largely a matter
of having time to analyze what appeared to be the component tasks in the
problems, and to ask myself in respect to each task, "How can I get around
the difficulties which kids seem to have here?" I had no conscious experience
of the generalizations of educational psychology suggesting a solution, but possibly these generalizations were active in whatever internal combustion chamber
creative fires burn. And when ideas came forth, such principles frequently
allowed a rapid assessment of practical potential. "Perhaps I should have the
children explicitly verbalize a rule for proceeding from a fact to be proved to
a class of propositions that would establish this fact," I would say to myself.
"Ah yes," I would answer, "this is consistent with the general efficacy of verbal
rules in steering the child's mental operation through tasks with a higher order
of perceptual complexity." And so the internal conversation went, some internal
process (possibly aided by psychological principles) throwing up suggestions; a
critical faculty dissecting and evaluating them in the light of known relationships.

My proposal that we should make our move through the methodologist is at
considerable odds with such solutions as: (*a*) core courses in academic psychology surrounded by satellite courses stressing application; (*b*) educational
psychologists combining in team fashion to acquaint teachers with their basic
research interests; and (*c*) educational psychologists attempting to make the
application to subject-matter areas themselves. The first two approaches seem
appropriate to graduate instruction in educational psychology. But I would

reject them all for teacher-training programs because, in general, neither psychologists nor educational psychologists are prepared to keep up with the rapid changes underway in the substantive fields now taught in our schools — and they are not, therefore, in a position to make imaginative applications. However, I think we can safely assume that the methodologist, if he so wished, is quite capable of assimilating in relatively short order the essential substance of our discipline.

An alliance with methodologists is just the initial step, however. I agree with the proposals that the teacher in training needs some kind of behavioral laboratory experience; my reasoning being that the procedural rules obtained from inventive methodology need strengthening through practice until they are at operational strength before the teacher enters the classroom. No doubt the practice-teaching experience — now largely an exercise in observing and practicing specific methodological rules — could be used to better advantage. For example, if the instructor in the educational psychology course is talking about categories of behavioral outcomes, and the methodologist is illustrating these in the teacher's substantive field, then the teacher himself should be instructed to identify and classify those activities observed in an ongoing lesson. Again, if the educational psychologist explains the theory of organizers, and the methodologist examines their application to a subject-matter field, then the teacher should be required to design and use one in his actual teaching. Much can be done in that way to give the teacher some experience in applying educational psychology principles.

I would also advocate exercises in behavioral change that employ much smaller groups of children, perhaps even one child. The fact is that the typical classroom teacher is so harried, and so far removed from the possibility of close observation and the precise control of the child's behavior, that he actually learns little about learning from his teaching experience. He is susceptible to the many myths about learning that permeate professional thinking; one of the most pernicious being that the present limitations on what the child learns in school can be safely attributed to the operation of some kind of natural law of development. Every teacher should have the experience of identifying some behavioral goal presently thought difficult or impossible for a child to attain, of performing a task analysis to reveal component skills, of attempting to teach these skills, and of evaluating the results. If the outcome were successful, as it would be with careful selection, the teacher would go into the classroom with a healthy respect for the potential of the child and an essential impatience with the limitations of mass education.

Not all such "lab" experiences need be of this dramatic kind. I have found that requiring experienced teachers to teach a concept to children of different age levels, while observing carefully both the kind and quality of props required to do so, fixed the essential attributes of stages of cognitive development in their minds far more precisely and permanently than reams of printed discourse. The results of these exercises, in attempting to produce specified behavioral goals, should figure prominently in the training institution's decision as to when the neophyte should be allowed to assume independent status in the classroom. The suggestion that the teacher should not be granted a certificate until he demonstrates that he can *change behavior* will sound abrasive in the ears of more genteel teacher educators, although it seems reasonable counsel.

Effecting a liaison with inventive methodologists will not be an easy task. The chief obstacle is that there is little incentive at present to improve methodology other than changing its content because the present methodology is quite capable of accomplishing the low-level behavioral goals we have set in education. By way of analogy, I would think that the typical group of children in today's schools could be compared to a group of runners who are required merely to keep pace with a slow-moving mechanical rabbit. If the trainer's methods are twenty percent less efficient than they might be, then the student may have to expend roughly twenty percent more effort, but he will have no trouble keeping up to the modest standard. The point is that efficient methodology only becomes critical (insofar as achievement is concerned) at the point of maximum effort, and we are far away from this point at the moment.

This may be thought to be a negative view. Let me, then, express the ultra-negative view. For some time a private hypothesis has been pressing inward upon my consciousness: certain attitudes are so ingrained in educators that the methodologist will be subjected to ridicule, scorn, and abuse in direct proportion to his ability to produce behavioral change over and above that now produced by the school. Having worked out a method for getting children aged eight to ten to solve problems which most students in the age group fourteen to sixteen found difficult — making a methodological improvement of the order of approximately two hundred percent on my scale — I was naturally ready to accept the plaudits and homage of teachers who were, I supposed, awaiting this beneficence. Unfortunately, commendation was not forthcoming but rather disdain. The typical reactions of teachers, when told of these results, were: "I think it is monstrous to force logical thinking on immature minds;" "all you will succeed in doing is warping the child's mind;" and this — which particularly grieves me — "what right have you to play God?" It is easy to single out the romantic naturalists, the embryological model theorists, the humanistic psychologists, or the Summerhillians as the official spokesmen for such viewpoints; but, I think there is a kind of ambivalence in most of us about the desirability of producing, via external control, dramatic changes in the behavior of a normal child.

In my view, until we are able to change the expectation of senior decision-makers and significant elements of the public, to enlist not only their support but also their *demand* for our inventive methodologies, the creator of such methodology must be prepared to be something of a martyr. Some may be willing to do this but although I once felt I might have made some modest contribution to the instruction of mathematics, I am too thin-skinned to endure sustained criticism, or even the interminable hassle which invariably arises at conferences between those who believe that in the final analysis inventive methodology means that one must be prepared to shape the child's behavior toward well-defined goals and those who would have few external controls, and would permit the child to develop according to his own needs and nature. Frustrated in the public sphere, I have retreated into retirement where at least I can try out my methods on my own children, imbibe the fermented juices of Niagara District grapes, and write parodies on educational practices and personalities. And if all attempts at honest employment fail, I can always make my living as a professor of educational psychology.

Commentary

L. B. Birch

When I accepted the assignment to respond to Floyd Robinson's paper I had one anxiety: I was afraid I might agree with everything he said and so be left with nothing to do except lamely underline his main points. My fears on this account were quite groundless for, apart from the fact that I think we do need a new approach to our job, I find myself in profound disagreement with what he has said. I think he is wrong in his diagnosis, his prognosis, and his treatment. I think he is also wrong when he so frequently tells us that we all agree with him.

When, for example, he says that we are *all* in agreement that something is drastically wrong with our current textbooks I beg to dissociate myself from this majority. I find that, on the whole, our current texts achieve a fair measure of success in reaching their declared goals though these are not what Robinson implies that the textbook writers are striving for.

The truth is, of course, that, with his tongue firmly in his cheek, he has used a technique which is more common in hustings than in a scientific meeting. He has erected a number of straw men and then kicked them to pieces. The picture he has drawn of current textbooks, for example, resembles nothing I have seen in my twenty years of university teaching. It is a very long time, if it ever was, since educational psychology was supposed to provide hints, tips, and recipes on how to teach this or that piece of knowledge. Rather, we have been concerned with the development of certain attitudes and high-level learning skills in our students. We hope that the teachers we train will see each teaching act as a tentative procedure, to be observed alertly and evaluated carefully. Then in the light of this evaluation we expect the teaching act to be modified and improved over and over again. To help him in this difficult, dynamic, unending task we, and the writers of the textbooks, have tried to provide the teacher with some of the means of evaluation, some of the criteria of success, and some of the models and general principles, which may guide the perceptive teacher in his search for tentative procedures.

I think the present-day textbooks have done a good job; yet, for reasons very different from those put forward by Robinson I think we do need a new approach to them.

For the purposes of today's exposition, Robinson has chosen to see the educational world fossilized in its present North American model. He talks, for example, of new curricula "which are placed intact in the teacher's hands"; of the textbook writer who incorporates into his text "the practice schedule which the teacher will actually use". He describes the curriculum-builder as some sinister artificer outside the school who devises "ultra-specific procedural rules" and "tells the teacher which book to buy, how to teach specific lessons" (down to specific questions to ask), "how much homework to assign, how to take it up, what to write on the board, what to put on the bulletin board, and so on."

His description of us is no more flattering: "the text, coupled with such folksy elaborations as may be offered by a none-too-well qualified instructor" will continue to represent the typical classroom teacher's acquaintance with our discipline for many years to come.

As one who has only recently come here from an alien culture I recognize this stereotype of Canadian education, much as I am beginning to recognize the faces of Canadian politicians in the newspaper cartoons. At the same time I also think I recognize all the signs of the beginning of a period of rapid change which, if I may judge from what I have seen happen in England during the past ten years, may lead to a totally different situation from the one Robinson has lampooned.

The first outcome of this change will, I predict, be the emergence of a much more professional teaching body in the schools. The teachers will demand *greater responsibility* and *control* over all aspects of their work. At the same time they will demand higher professional standards of their members. The first casualty will be the curriculum builder, for responsibility for what is taught, and how, will rest firmly with the school principal and his staff. If outside experts like subject specialists or child psychologists go into the schools they will do so as consultants, by invitation of the principal and not by right.

"The book for the grade," approved by somebody outside the school for use in all the schools in an area, will go and be replaced by a multiplicity of different books, journals, catalogues, encyclopedia, and such. This change will be paralleled by a change in content and in method. We may, especially with younger children, see a great diminution in the use of the set lesson where thirty children sit facing north and one adult stands facing south. Instead, children will devote a great deal of their time in library- and laboratory-situations actively seeking the solutions to worthwhile questions for themselves. The emphasis in the teacher's job will have transferred from the sort of task which Robinson describes as characteristic of school learning, and which "deals with hierarchically organized, eminently comprehensible, sequentially related bodies of ideas which are learned systematically over a period of time . . ." The new emphasis will be on the *way* learning takes place and on the development of high-level learning skills.

By this I mean the ability to recognize a problem, to assess its importance and its ramifications, then quickly to find out what other people have thought and done about this and related problems. Then, after having evaluated what has been discovered a synthesis is to be provided, which can be communicated to others and form a basis for further action. While the emphasis may be on learning skills, there is no reason to suppose that the skills and knowledge so laboriously taught in the past will not be equally well learned, as a bonus, in the newer classroom methods.

We shall be teaching teachers to fit into this school climate, and as Cronbach pointed out in a paper in the Bulletin of the British Psychological Society in 1956, a major cause of change in teacher-training methods lies in the disparity between the teaching methods advocated and those actually used in our courses of instruction to teachers in training. If the schools go over to the sort of programs I have suggested, it will no longer do for us to base the bulk of our teaching on the lecture and the textbook of the course. We can no longer continue to examine the regurgitated content of textbook and notebook by machine-scored multiple-choice answers.

I think we, who are engaged in teacher preparation, must teach in the way our best teachers will teach. We shall come down off our rostra and with our students we shall delineate problems to solve and areas of information to illumine. Then, as leaders and technical advisers we shall allow our students free access to the sources of information they need and help them to develop for themselves the skills they need. They will work singly and in groups and will come together in plenary session to *hear from each other* what has been discovered and to discuss its significance. To do this we shall need a great deal more help than the textbook at present gives us, though it may often prove an excellent starting point for wider excursions.

I think we need books at a series of difficulty levels, and with some new characteristics. At the first level I think we need a number of very elementary, very short, readable texts which can be read with ease by students who are contemplating teaching as a career but who have not yet entered upon a course of study. These would give a bird's eye view of the whole field of education: how it developed, how other countries do it, the function of the schools, etc., as well as those areas related to psychology. These would perhaps be mainly natural histories and would be without footnotes, references, or disputatious material.

For the course proper we need a few general texts — and I see no special reason for changing our present ones beyond the normal need of revision. But in addition we need much more if we are to modernize our teaching. We need a very large number of monographs separately published on specific topics. Each should be written by an expert in the particular field. Each should be as short as possible but should be complete and have full scientific support and references. Production should be cheap.

The advantages for the *teacher* are obvious. Given enough of these, a class of students can be let loose on a fact-finding, problem-solving learning experience in the knowledge that they are not going to be held up for want of material. More advanced students could expect to move straight from these monographs to journals and other primary sources.

The *publisher* will find much less delay in getting his scripts since each author is writing in his own area and will probably have all his data at his finger tips. It is much easier to get an author to produce a few chapters on his own field of interest than it is to get him to write a whole book.

The *author* will get satisfaction out of writing what he *wants* to write and not having to give up a great deal of time to do it. Since the books are so small he will be able to revise at frequent intervals instead of having to go through the series of deceptions of reprinting and revising, with minimal revisions, which the present system of big texts imposes.

Obviously, a problem-solving approach to teaching, with a great deal of personal responsibility on the student for organizing his own studies, inevitably leads to a breakdown in traditional curriculum boundaries. Is it then too much for an outsider, who is married to a "course" and "credit" approach to university learning, to ask whether anything should and could be done to allow students to cross some of the boundaries of the courses in our own discipline, if not to permit them to venture into the neighboring areas of sociology, philosophy, anthropology, and so on?

Research in the Preparation of Teachers:
Background Factors that Must Be Considered

J. M. Stephens

I want to examine some primitive background factors that are always at work whenever education or schooling is in progress.

A number of our colleagues are planning to use classroom outcomes as the criterion to test curricular innovations in teacher education. They will use several different approaches in teacher education and then, some years later, they will try to see if there is any difference between the pupils taught by the teachers with the different preparations. The audacity of this straightforward approach is to be admired. For illustration, one group of prospective teachers would learn about educational psychology by the traditional textbook course. The other group is to be prepared by a series of mini-teaching experiences designed to provide maximum transfer to the regular classroom. Later the people in both groups will be put in charge of classrooms, and the researchers will see if there is any difference in the pupils' accomplishment.

Consider the powerful background factors that will be at work in both groups. These factors will be working on the pupils taught by both groups of teachers. Some of these common background factors will operate through the teachers themselves. Others will work directly on the pupils. Taken together they may well push the accomplishment of both groups of pupils to a very high level. And the net effectiveness of either treatment will have to emerge from the findings above this exalted base line.

Our first consideration will be the basic forces and inclinations in the prospective teacher himself. He does not come to us as an inert, empty memory drum, waiting to be programmed in any manner that we see fit. He comes to us instead with a host of powerful pedagogical tendencies that he has acquired through centuries of human evolution, and through his own experiences.

These built-in pedagogical tendencies stem from the long period of human evolution during which minimal education was a grim survival necessity. Human beings have been able to out-compete other groups only because of the sustained and dedicated furthering of the kind of behavior ordinarily nurtured by schools and by the extended family. Let me say in passing that I do not make the same claim for the present elaborate educational establishment. I am not sure that this amount of schooling is necessary for survival. Indeed there is some danger that, carried to this extreme, it may become an evolutionary hazard. In going through college or university, a student remains in the state of an infant for an amazing length of time. The adolescent traumata, with their hostilities and resentments, are continued through what should be, in some areas, his most productive years. It is one thing for a few expendable weirdos to be subjected to this excessive prolongation of infancy and to be permitted to concentrate on their own development instead of the world's, but things may be different when this prolongation becomes the mode and when adolescent hostilities and sustained introspection become incorporated into the attitudes of *most* of our young adults. We may well be overrun by some culture in which the stupendous energy of youth is directed to real problems and is not spent exclusively in attacking the annoying idiosyncrasies of fuddy-duddy university administrations.

However much we may question the survival value of current educational activities, there can be no similar doubt about the value of the minimal schooling thousands of years ago. Such minimal schooling was an evolutionary necessity.

To provide such minimal schooling, I have maintained, our race has evolved a cluster of non-deliberate, spontaneous tendencies that would dependably produce a modicum of schooling even on the part of those who have no intention to teach. These spontaneous tendencies: to speak of what we know, to react to the behavior of others, to point out the moral, and to supply the answer that temporarily eludes the other fellow exist and are most powerful. We tell secrets that we have resolved not to tell. We give ourselves up to the police by recounting our criminal exploits. We drive away our friends by talking endlessly of our hobbies, our trips, or our operations. We correct the erroneous statements of our associates and accept the resulting risk of becoming a social outcast. Unless prevented by powerful taboos we incessantly point the moral, and emit strings of "I told you so's." We yearn to make up for the maladroit behavior of others, to get our hands on that spoiled brat, to grasp the wheel from the fumbling driver, to blurt out answers that seem to elude the contestant on the quiz program.

These powerful tendencies, so compulsive, so prevalent, so frequently noted, so often deplored, must have had some function. When given relatively free play, as when an adult associates with helpless children, they have, all by themselves, generated a substantial amount of schooling.

If our prospective teachers are randomly assigned to the two treatments considered, they will, of course, be comparable with respect to these spontaneous tendencies. Merely to control them we need do nothing special. To get a measure of the effectiveness of these forces, however, we need two control groups. One of these should consist of children not exposed to any teacher. The other should be made up of children who associate with young adults who have no intention to teach, but who are comparable to our two groups with respect to the spontaneous tendencies mentioned.

I contend that some teaching would result even if an adult were merely to baby-sit for half an hour a day with growing children. However, the prospective teachers in our groups not only have a normal quota of the important spontaneous tendencies but they also have a sense of mission. Unlike the young adults just specified, the prospective teachers of our group know that they are supposed to teach. Their sense of mission, even without any training, might produce considerable instruction. Consequently we need another control group of young adults who, like the other groups, are well endowed with the spontaneous tendencies, but who are also told that they are expected to teach.

Our two prospective groups of teachers are to receive training in psychology. The course content may be important, yet by giving the training, we are suggesting to the prospective teachers that it is important for them to acquire skill in the art of teaching. We are also saying that the psychology courses may make a difference in how one teaches. The training, regardless of the content, sensitizes them to psychological insights and teaching skills. This sensitization may also affect their performance. Apart from the content and the sensitization, the confidence which results from the conviction that they have received the training they needed may also have an impact on their teaching.

To take care of this background factor of sensitization, or of being alerted to the importance of a course or curriculum, we need still another control group exposed to pseudo-instruction. This group should think they are getting training in psychology but they should not get real training. They should be exposed to all the trappings of instruction, but not the content.

I have implied that one should have a separate control group of background factors. Of course, one could take care of things merely by making sure that the two training groups were comparable in each of these background matters. And then, if one found a significant advantage in the gains of the pupils taught by one group of teachers, one could credit that superiority to the difference in the training. But, unless one escapes the fate of the research already reported by Mitzell, Medley, and others, one will probably not get a significant difference. And, in that case one may well want to know if the training variable interacts with any of the background factors, and if so, how.

Telling a teacher that he should think about his teaching, for instance, may be like telling the centipede to consider how he runs. But this factor could be offset by one training approach. The other training program may interact only slightly with this background effect, but may have a definite interaction with another background factor. All this could result in a dead heat for the main effects, even though the offsetting interactions were both positive and important.

This stress on background factors is inherently mixed up with a very cautious attitude toward either research or major reform in teacher education. The new program must prove its superiority by showing a different departure from the very lofty base line produced by the background factors. The background factors may already have pushed this base line of competence in teaching to the point of diminishing returns. Consequently we would need an enormous improvement in training procedures to show any appreciable net advantage.

Whenever we are dealing with young children, we must regard maturation as one of the background factors to be taken into account before the net effect of instruction can be assessed. Whenever a young child is subjected to instruction, several things may happen. Obviously, he may be learning but he may also merely be growing old enough to profit from the instruction. The presence of these two processes makes it difficult to know just how much has been accomplished by the program of instruction. We see clearly, for instance, that, after six years of instruction, the twelve-year old can read much better than he could six years ago. But does this improvement come entirely from the six years of instruction? Probably not. During this time, the pupil was also increasing his ability to learn. If we had waited until this ability had developed, he might have acquired all this mastery in one or two years.

In general, the literature points to the fact that, in the case of young children, a given amount of instruction is more effective when applied to an older child than when applied to a younger child (Baer, 1958; Hall, 1963; Tyler, 1964). Much of the change that takes place during the period of instruction can properly be attributed to this salutary maturation.

It must be remembered that we are dealing with the influence of maturation on general scholastic development. The evidence is more than adequate to justify caution on the part of the researcher. This evidence, however, should not induce the practitioner to go overboard in following its implications. From Piagetian theory and from the data on imprinting there is much to suggest that maturation is a two-way force. Not only can we start too early, but we can wait too long. Even when the evidence points unambiguously to the advantages of "waiting," moreover, practical considerations may outweigh the gains to be had from deferring instruction.

Among the background influences that play a pronounced part in the scholastic growth of young children we must include the many out-of-school agencies. The school is by no means the only agency that acts on the child while he is acquiring the maturity necessary for learning. During his maturing years he is continually confronted by academic materials in his experiences outside the school. Parental chitchat assails him with concepts and factual information. Picture magazines, books, and billboards display letters and words to him. Ubiquitous television confronts him with words portraying the glories of various cosmetics while the voice of the model provides the auditory counterpart of the printed symbols.

It is not surprising that children learn a good deal about academic matters apart from the school. Many first graders, about to be exposed to formal schooling, already know much about the world (Huck, 1955). Grade 3 children, just about to undertake formal instruction in social studies for the first time, already know about one third of the materials prepared for their education (Kaltsounis, 1964).

As a rough index of some of these background factors, we could use the socio-economic status of parents. As a more inclusive index we could use the child's intellectual status as he first enters school. This intellectual attainment must come from a cluster of out-of-school forces, biological and cultural. Taken together, these indexes will account for almost sixty percent of the variance in educational attainment to be found between schools (Kemp, 1955).

The maturational and other out-of-school forces continue to act during the period the pupil is receiving instruction. As far as instruction is concerned, moreover, there are other background factors stemming from the school itself. The specific instruction takes place in a general setting, and, it is in this setting that these other background factors which contribute to academic proficiency are found.

Even as he approaches the school's doors, the child is probably influenced by the very reputation of the school itself. To some extent he must be aware of the school as an institution concerned about academic matters. Just as churches are places where one foregoes boisterous play and thinks religious thoughts, so schools are places where it behooves one to have an eye to his academic manners (Stephens, 1933). The school is a place where one cannot take liberties with grammar, spelling, and mathematics.

There is, then, a general force that arises from the school's reputation, and which persists throughout the child's day. Even in other settings, academic matters will take on additional significance because the school, by its sheer reputation, has called attention to their importance.

The sensitization thus induced is not as marked as the sensitization that takes place after instruction has begun. In discussing the training of prospective teachers, we pointed out that the mere act of instruction says in effect, "This specific material is important." This influence, held to be important in the training of teachers, is also at work in the pupils.

To see how these general sanctions work with young children, even in the absence of meaningful instruction, an experiment in which the class is learning the location of certain key cities in the United States would be a good illustration. The pupils know that they are supposed to be learning this material. The teacher flashes the name of a city on the screen. A few seconds later he flashes the name of the state in which the city is to be found. It happens, however, that the projector is out of focus and the images are so blurred that the pupils cannot decipher them. Under these circumstances the pupils would acquire no information, nor would they be able to determine whether or not they had thought of the right state. But they could not fail to be impressed with the fact that cities do have a state location, and that somebody thinks this is important.

Some aspects of this hypothetical illustration were actually employed by Entwisle (1961) in an attempt to test the influence of sanctions, or of set, or enhancement of stimuli. As in the hypothetical illustration, the children were supposed to be learning the states in which certain key cities were located. Two groups of children was tested on the state locations of some fifty-eight cities. The children in one group were then given three separate lessons on the locations of *half* of these cities. The lessons were distributed over a period of two months. During the times that these pupils were assembled for instruction, a control group was also assembled but spent the time reading in the library.

Compared to the control group, the instructed group did show a significant gain on the cities that they had studied during the training sessions. But, again compared to the control group, they also made a significant gain on the other cities *they had never studied.* As might be expected, however, the gain on the unstudied items was less than the gain on the items presented during the practice periods.

By calling attention to a certain class of items and by implying that pupils should know them, the school can induce some growth. To bring about this growth, one would have to make sure that the pupils know about the items in question. In the experiment just cited, the material was of the type that pupils would probably come across in their out-of-school experience. For more esoteric items it would be necessary to go to some trouble to arrange for the necessary encounters.

After some growth has been induced by the very general sanctions supplied by the school, additional growth is produced by specific instruction. The pupils who actually receive instruction will ordinarily be found to learn more than those who are merely led to believe that the material is important. But the latter do learn something. Not all the observed growth can be attributed to the detailed processes of instruction.

To illustrate the combined effects of all these background factors as they affect the pupils being taught, we might consider some classic data reported by Courtis (1949). The report came from a school system in which Grade 8 children were taught to spell the word "sincerely." The word "customary" was not taught at all. Children were tested on both of these words from Grade 2 through Grade 9. Each year there was a steady increase in the number of children able to spell both words, even before "sincerely" was taught. In Grade 8 the pupils' mastery of "sincerely" spurted ahead, suggesting the role of specific instruction. Mastery of "customary" continued to increase at the regular rate through Grades 8 and 9. By Grade 9 the advantage for "sincerely" had dropped off, and the mastery of the two words was indistinguishable. Throughout the period from Grade 2 to Grade 9 there was a marked increase for both words.

Except, then, for a short period of specific instruction, the pupils learned the words at about the same rate. During the seven-year period, the mastery of both words was facilitated by the pronounced increase in general maturity. Both words were probably encountered in out-of-school experiences and in casual experiences within the school. Because of its reputation, and because of the general expression of its concerns, the school had given the impression that "spelling is important." This emphasis was applied to both words. Because of all these general background factors, both words were increasingly mastered as the children grew older. When specific instruction was applied to one of them, there was a transient advantage for the word being taught.

As indicated earlier, whenever two groups of prospective teachers are to be trained by different methods, the superiority of one method over the other must show itself when both are imposed on background factors common to both approaches. Some of these background factors reside in the persons of the prospective teachers and in the conditions of their instruction. Other background factors, as indicated, reside in the nature of the pupils to be taught by our prospective teachers and in the inevitable conditions surrounding the instruction of these pupils.

In planning or in testing our training programs, we should remember that we are engaged in a process similar to the shaping of a hedge to a preconceived pattern in which our deliberate efforts must be geared to the age-old botanical forces at work. There is no one-to-one correspondence between the amount of effort we exert and the result achieved. Excessive industry could even be ruinous. Here we would be less likely to hear the outraged shriek of the efficiency expert who sees us loafing for two months of the year, our expensive unused equipment stored in the potting shed, while we wait for the organism to recover from the treatment we have inflicted.

Our deliberate efforts ought to be applied to these powerful background factors that were there first and are still at work. When adequately studied, they should give us a clearer picture of the high base line from which our deliberate innovations must produce a departure if they are to show a net effect. More important, when we incorporate these factors into our research designs, we should be able to determine how each of these forces interacts with the treatment we are about to apply.

References

BAER, C. J.   The school progress and adjustment of underage and overage students. *Journal of Educational Psychology,* 1958 (Feb.), **49**, 17-19.

COURTIS, S. A.   The rate of growth makes a difference. *Phi Delta Kappan,* 1949, **30**, 316-323.

ENTWISLE, D. R.   Attensity: Factors of specific set in school learning. *Harvard Educational Review,* 1961 (Winter), **31**, 84-101.

HALL, C. V.   Does entrance age affect achievement? *Elementary School Journal,* 1963 (Apr.), **63**, 391-396.

HUCK, C.   Children learn from their culture. *Educational Leadership,* 1955 (Dec.), **13**, 171-175.

KALTSOUNIS, T. A.   A study concerning third graders' knowledge of social studies content prior to instruction. *Journal of Educational Research,* 1964 (Mar.), **57**, 345-349.

KEMP, L. C. D.   Environmental and other characteristics determining attainment in primary schools. *British Journal of Educational Psychology,* 1955, **25**, 67-77.

STEPHENS, J. M.   *The influence of the school on the individual.* Ann Arbor, Michigan: Edwards Bros., 1933.

TYLER, F. T.   Issues related to readiness to learn. In *Theories of learning and instruction.* Sixty-third Yearbook of the National Society for the Study of Education. Part I. Chicago: University of Chicago Press, 1964. Pp. 210-239.

Commentary

John Macdonald

A curious notion came to me as I was reading J. M. Stephens's paper — that, if populism had ever found it necessary to invent an educational psychology, what was invented would have been very much along his lines. It is clear — to me, at any rate — that Stephens thinks better of ordinary men and less well of the highly educated than do most of his fellows; that he distrusts what used to be called book-larnin; that he blurs the differences between teaching and casually informative talking, and between learning in school and learning out of school; that he is prepared to stand by "common sense" as a guide through the intricacies of the study of behavior. For Stephens, the educational system in North America divided naturally into two parts: a useful part, generally to be equated with the less advanced levels of instruction, which is the repository of the natural wisdom of the race; and an increasingly parasitic and hypertrophied part, generally to be equated with the more advanced levels of instruction, which is already weakening the fiber of our civilization. He believes that schools are capable of achieving only limited and rather simple purposes, and that more ambitious goals are ill-advised. Finally, he regards the task of improving teacher education as an enormously difficult one, especially since he favors only "a moderate amount of professional training." The last phrase is taken from the 1956 edition of Stephens' *Educational Psychology*, in which he illustrates the point by quoting the story of the shrewd Yankee farmer who, upon being urged to buy a set of books on farming, replied, "Shucks! I ain't farming half as well as I know how to, now." (This, if I may say so, is a very populist story.)

With most of what Stephens has to say I have considerable difficulty in agreeing. His caution and willingness to find unsuspected benefits in the untouched present remind me of those expositions of neo-liberal social ideology so popular a few years ago (such as what is put forward in Bell's *The End of Ideology* and Popper's *The Open Society and Its Enemies*; the Oakeshott version of political science and the Lipset version of sociology, which have strongly affected the study of educational administration but have not so far had much apparent influence on educational psychology). I must add, however, that the paper is remarkable for one striking perception: the modern school is still a relatively primitive institution, in which learning and instruction follow essentially the same paths that they have followed for many generations in informal social settings. In other words, although the school sets learning and instruction in a special context, what happens within that context is contiguous with what happens in more casual social interchanges, and the difference between teaching and the directed talk characteristic of ordinary social confrontation is much less than is commonly supposed.

I believe that this perception is essentially correct, but it leads me to my own set of interpretations. Stephens obviously has in mind a preferred role for the school rather similar to that of the nightwatchman state in nineteenth-century liberal thought, and regards any claims to additional potency as dangerously neglectful of the evolutionary needs of human society, and perhaps suspects them of opening the gate to the more practical barbarians: "We may well be overrun by some culture in which the stupendous energy of youth is directed to real problems." However, my reading of the contemporary situation is that continued dependence on a model of schooling given to us by nature is a very inadequate approach to the problems that man has created for himself in his attempts to overcome nature, and that the school must disentangle itself from non-deliberative milieus, and assign much more carefully chosen means to the service of much more explicitly formulated ends. I would even go so far as to say that, while these non-deliberate, spontaneous tendencies to inform (and, presumably, to receive information) of which Stephens speaks, certainly exist. They are likely to interfere with, rather than support, the process of education which is not a naturally given process. It cannot be viewed simply as a form of evolutionary adaptation to a hostile environment.

I should have thought, too, that "the long period of human evolution" had left its mark on us in other ways besides those listed by Stephens. Human evolution in the natural environment seems to have been distinguished by the conservation of options, and one would therefore suspect that human beings possess built-in antipedagogical tendencies as well as built-in pedagogical tendencies. If we are to accept this notion of inherited psychological tendency at all, then one kind of tendency appears just as reasonable as the other: the rejection of the informal instruction, and the unwillingness to display or share information, may also have survival value. Certainly anthropologists have been much struck by the widely differing patterns of social interaction, with their implications for ease of exchange of information, to be found among primitive cultures. It is unjustifiable to suppose that we are the direct descendants of cultures with liberal information-sharing patterns, since almost all early civilization appears to have adopted a hierarchical model of social organization which placed severe restrictions on the free flow of information.

However, I am willing to accept, up to a point, that the school is in origin a natural extension of various informal social arrangements for passing on information to others. Yet origin does not prescribe function; and one may acknowledge that the school is still the prisoner of Stephens's "non-deliberate, spontaneous tendencies" without approving of this state of affairs. I am perfectly ready to endorse his pessimistic views of the capabilities of educational research, *in the setting with which he has provided us*; but are we bound to take this setting for granted? Man, as well as being a creature of nature, transcends it. But he cannot do so unless at some time what happens in the school begins to run counter to the promptings of custom and natural tradition, and starts to oppose nature. At that point educational research and teacher training at once assume real importance and acquire a demonstrable value. Thus, in order for teacher training to come into its own, it is necessary that a task definition be in use which sharply distinguishes between teaching and whatever casual instruction, even of an intended nature, goes on in informal out-of-school contexts. (Just in passing, I should add that it is also necessary to distinguish between teaching and therapy, to the confusion of which educational reformers are especially prone.)

If educational research is to flourish, it is necessary that the curriculum be properly regarded as an artificial creation that requires the invention of a methodology and cannot rest in the shadow of an outworn equation between education and life. The curious mishmash that now passes under the name of educational psychology, and on which Ausubel properly comments in his paper, is a logical, not a substantive derivation. There are schools; what goes on in schools is formally defined as education; obviously, psychology must have something to do with education; hence, a field of study called educational psychology must exist. But in fact educational psychology is still a discipline in search of a field. A recognition of this somewhere below the level of full awareness has driven those who call themselves educational psychologists in two directions. Some have ventured into the human relations/personal development jungle, where they show signs of succumbing to nightmares; others have retreated to the reluctant arms of the parent discipline, and live in an uncomfortable half-world. The present relationship of educational psychology to the school is indeed like the relationship of politics to the economic structure in a number of underdeveloped countries; before it can be effective, there has to be a reorganization of application. Educational psychologists, therefore, cannot commit themselves to the present school without destroying the prospects of development for their own discipline.

Stephens has given us (in passing, and by implication, rather than directly), a penetrating account of the pitfalls that lie in wait for educational researchers. My essential response is that, if these are inevitable pitfalls, then the future for educational psychology is dim indeed. But I do not think that it is so. I think that his discussion takes for granted the purposes, the organization, and the methodology of a particular type of the school, that this type has little to support it except a very lengthy tradition, and that other types of a much more rational and consciously designed sort can, in principle at least, be generated easily.

Stalking Beasts and Swatting Flies: Comments on Educational Psychology and Teacher Training

Philip W. Jackson

This has not been an easy paper to write, though I had expected it to be when I agreed to write it. I have been thinking a lot about teachers and teaching recently and I also have been teaching educational psychology for several years. So I thought it would be a simple matter to put a few of my ideas down on paper. In fact, I even looked forward to the task because I saw it as a chance to clarify one or two vague notions that have been in the back of my mind for some time. For example, I am convinced that we have to understand more about the relative roles of belief and knowledge as they function in teacher-training programs and as they give shape to what teachers do. The more I become involved with teachers and with teaching the more impressed I become with how much depends on what people believe and how little depends on what they know.

It was with high hopes, therefore, that I began my writing. But it was not long before I realized that I had bitten off more than I could chew, at least within the time and space limitations available to me. Belief and knowledge, it turns out, are rather slippery concepts, even in the hands of professional philosophers.

Each time I began to explore a topic that I had looked forward to writing on, whether it be belief and knowledge in teacher training or inputs and outputs, I discovered that I had a tiger by the tail and not enough in the way of hunting equipment, or courage, to bring him home. But in between my encounters with big game I was constantly annoyed, as are most hunters, by the buzz of insects, in the form of bothersome questions and side issues that kept intruding into my thoughts while I was trying to concentrate on what I believed to be more important matters. I never did manage to get rid of these queries and digressions, but since I also failed to bag anything more impressive I might as well let them have their day. I have little else to talk about today except my experience as a swatter of flies.

The first question that kept pricking my conscience as I thought about the conference was: Does it really *matter* how we teach educational psychology to teachers, or whether we bother to teach it at all? Brushing aside the obvious answer, that it matters very much to those of us who make a living out of it, I think we must confess that no one really *knows* the answer to this question, though many of us have strong *beliefs* about the matter. The most direct way of answering this question would be to demonstrate that one way of teaching educational psychology, as contrasted with some other way, would produce

65

a better crop of teachers. Yet, as we all know, such evidence has not yet been produced, nor, in my opinion, is it likely to be.

The chief reason for my pessimism, in addition to my awareness of the difficulty of identifying a superior teacher, stems from a consideration of the vastness and complexity of human experience as contrasted with the narrowness and simplicity of something called "taking a course in educational psychology." Most people, when they begin to teach, are already in their early twenties. They have lived for 180,000 hours or so, of which only fifty or a hundred have been spent in the study of educational psychology. They look forward, with luck, to forty years or more of teaching, or about 40,000 hours of professional work, all of which will be embedded in something like 400,000 hours of extra-curricular activity.

Certainly each of those hours of pre-service experience is not equally influential in shaping a teacher's professional style. Surely it is reasonable to hope that four years of college training does something to a person which stays with him and is apparent to the outside world for the rest of his days. It is even reasonable to expect that certain *parts* of that total college experience are more influential than are other parts. Accordingly, we might argue that the hours spent in studying educational psychology are more likely to have an impact on future performance than would a comparable period of time spent in studying audiovisual education or methods of teaching social studies. But when we reduce our focus to the scope of a course or two — particularly ones where content is not sharply differentiated from the rest of the student's life — the likelihood of finding traces of this experience in the student's behavior throughout the years ahead becomes extremely remote. Thus, to imagine that the infinitesimal investment of energy expended in the study of educational psychology will have a perceptible and enduring effect on the forty years of teaching toward which our students are moving is to indulge in fanciful expectations at best, and presumptuous ones at worst.

A less direct way of assessing the long-term impact of educational psychology is by asking teachers whether it has been helpful to them in their work. When this measure of worth is applied, the results, almost invariably, are encouraging to those who teach the subject. For example, after questioning a sizeable number of graduates, Herbert and Williams report that educational psychology is seen as one of the most valuable of all the courses in teacher training. Other surveys have come up with similar findings and the interesting thing is that it does not seem to matter where the course was taken, how it was structured, or what textbook was used! Apparently, the majority of students, when sufficiently removed from the experience itself, will testify to the benefits of studying educational psychology, no matter what.

Although we probably should be pleased by this type of evidence, I am always a little troubled by it. First, because I know that people have a way of believing that experiences designed to be good for them *are* good for them. The majority of church-attenders probably believe that their devotional activities make them more honest and upright than they would otherwise be, but there is little evidence to support these claims. I am more inclined to believe that their perception of the benefits derived is somewhat distorted by what they have been led to expect. Similarly, it is true with teachers' praise of educational psychology.

A second reason why I cannot take the applause of teachers too seriously is that I am not terribly impressed by the quality of the other professional courses in their training. As a graduate of a state teachers college, I can testify to the hours of tedium during which I was forced to sit through countless dull courses taught by dull instructors. To say that Educational Psychology 205 was among the best of the batch is really not saying much. We must ask what is the baseline against which teachers assess the relative merits of educational psychology? If the total quality of their professional training is low, and I suspect it is in many institutions, we cannot allow ourselves to become too elated by the relative popularity of our specialty.

Even if we cannot show that the study of educational psychology makes a real and enduring difference in teachers' behavior and even if we have some misgivings about the fact that teachers themselves are willing to applaud our efforts, we cannot afford to conclude that it makes no difference whether or how we teach our subject. We will probably continue to "do our thing," as the hippies say, and we might as well try to do it as best we can.

In the absence of clear-cut effectiveness, we are forced to apply other criteria in choosing among the many ways of structuring educational psychology. Our appeal must be broadly rational rather than narrowly empirical. Clearly, there are many ways of structuring educational psychology, as evidenced by the plethora of textbooks in the field and the variety of practices described by John Herbert and Donald Williams in their recent survey. It is difficult to choose the best, although I believe that every textbook writer and every curriculum designer is obliged to explain why he believes he has a corner on the truth.

I look forward, therefore, to a continuation of controversy in educational psychology for a long time. It is this state of affairs that prompts publishers to design attractive dust jackets and to throw cocktail parties at professional conventions. I, for one, would hate to see them disappear.

Another suspicion that kept creeping into my mind was that educational psychologists, as a group, seem to honor research more than thought. It seems strange, I admit, to conceive of research and thinking as separable activities for, ideally, they are both natural manifestations of an inquiring mind. But, unfortunately, research may be done thoughtlessly, just as thinking may soar free of empirical moorings. Among educational psychologists, it seems that nonempirical thinking is a far more grievous fault than thoughtless empirical research. I am led to this conclusion by several different observations.

Consider, for example, the articles that get published in our professional journals, particularly the *Journal of Educational Psychology* and the *American Educational Research Journal*. Suppose you had written a thoughtful essay on the teaching process, would you submit it to either of these publications? Perhaps you would, but as a consulting editor of one of them I can tell you that the chances of its being accepted are mighty small. And this state of affairs holds not only for the two journals in question. In fact, a fourth-rate piece of empirical research stands a much better chance of finding its way into print than does a first- or second-rate article that contains no hard data.

It could be argued, of course, that the publications I have named are clearly "research" journals and, therefore, the author of a "think piece" is foolish even to try to break into them. His efforts are more properly suited to the pages of the *School Review*, the *Harvard Educational Review*, or *Teachers College Record*. These are among the leading repositories of "soft" educational thought in North America. But such an argument misses the point, that the field of educational psychology is implicitly defined by its "official" publications. The graduate student or the aspiring young faculty member who turns to such publications in search of directions, or merely to strengthen his sense of professional identification, comes away with little doubt concerning the proper activity of an educational psychologist. "Do research!" the pages shout. "It doesn't matter too much what kind of research as long as the data are handled appropriately. Data, quantifiable data of course, are essential. Moreover, don't spend too much space justifying the importance of the problem you are working. Stick to the facts, and keep the discussion short."

These implicit admonitions do more than define the format of a successful article — i.e., one that is accepted for publication — they also indirectly sanction a particular style of working and thinking about problems in educational psychology. Not only is the non-quantifiable left out in the cold, but form overpowers content, and technique is left to rule the roost. The result is a plethora of technically adequate but trivial exercises, lacking in cumulative significance, and unconnected, except by the wildest stretch of imagination, to the concerns of the practitioner. A sure way of arousing laughter from an audience of teachers is to say, "Here are the problems that keep educational psychologists awake at night," and then read aloud from the table of contents of any recent issue of an educational research journal.

In my more cynical moods this state of affairs leads me to conclude that the major function of research in education is to advance the careers of educational researchers. I realize that this conclusion is a bit unfair, first, because there are many dedicated and thoughtful workers in the field, and, second, because similar conditions probably hold in other areas of research endeavor. But if academic degrees and promotions were based on criteria other than demonstrated research competence I suspect that the authors of many of these "contributions to the literature" would be spending their afternoons on golf courses. Both the worlds of sport and education would likely benefit from such a change.

In case my complaints sound too much like those of a rejected author, let me hasten to assure you that this is not the case. I have managed to "make the scene," as my adolescent friends say, a reasonable number of times and will probably continue to do so. In a sense, then, I have helped to perpetuate the very conditions I here deplore. But, strangely enough, if I had not done so I would not be legitimate in the eyes of my colleagues.

Another symptom of the low estate into which thinking has fallen in our field is the popularity of data-gathering instruments and techniques. Design a test, invent an observational device, construct an attitude scale, and it will soon be in use around the country by researchers who had not previously shown the slightest interest in the substantive problem that occasioned the invention. Indeed, the original purpose of the technique often gets lost in the shuffle and it becomes employed in the pursuit of ends for which it was not designed. Instruments developed for the exploration of a problem area are used for purposes of evaluation and personnel selection long before anyone really knows what they measure. The important question seems to be: Does it produce data? If so, what are we waiting for?

Not only is there a rush to use data-gathering procedures before they have been fully developed, there is also a tendency to seize upon a small number of these procedures and elevate them to a level of prominence far beyond that intended by their developers. Two techniques, specifically related to problems of teacher training, might serve as example: interaction analysis and microteaching.

Those of you who attended the last AERA convention in Chicago cannot have failed to notice how many investigators were employing some variation of Flanders' technique and how many more were setting out to take five-minute video-tapes of their subjects in action. In fact, in a few happy instances both techniques were being used by the same researcher. An observer who did not know what an I/D ratio was or who was uncomfortable with talk of "feedback" and "microlessons" must have felt very much out of place at many of the sessions.

The issue is not whether these two techniques have merit — I assume they are both very useful in special contexts — but whether their widespread use in teacher training and research is not an act of convenience, a reflection of our unwillingness to take the time to think about what we are doing. We clearly need to move closer to what really goes on when teachers confront students, and both interaction analysis and microteaching may offer us a way of doing that. But I wondered, as I listened to some of their reports, how many of these investigators would bother to take time away from loading their cameras and inspecting their interaction matrices to heed the words of the critic who said:

It ought to go without saying (unfortunately, it does not in all cases) that criticism should be directed to making the professional student thoughtful about his work in the light of principles, rather than to induce in him a recognition that certain special methods are good, and certain other special methods bad. At all events, no greater travesty of real intellectual criticism can be given than to set a student to teaching a brief number of lessons, have him under inspection in practically all the time of every lesson, and then criticize him almost, if not quite, at the very end of each lesson, upon the particular way in which that particular lesson has been taught, pointing out elements of failure and of success. Such methods of criticism may be adapted to giving a training-teacher command of some of the knacks and tools of the trade, but are not calculated to develop a thoughtful and independent teacher.

The critic, incidentally, was John Dewey and his remarks were written in 1904.[1] But, then, who needs Dewey? What has *he* published lately?

One more swat and I'll be gone. The question can be phrased in many ways, but they all boil down to the general query: What do educational psychologists have to offer teachers anyway? This is rather different from my first question, which had to do with whether the teaching of educational psychology led to an observable difference in teachers' behavior. Leaving aside, for now, the effects of our efforts, I shall examine the nature of our contribution to the process of becoming a teacher.

Some people seem to believe that educational psychologists are the only professionals who are engaged in serious thinking and research related to the processes of teaching and learning as they occur in schools. But this is absurd. When I think of those among my contemporaries whose writings about education excite me, I come up with a curious collection of philosophers, curriculum experts, psychologists, anthropologists, sociologists, and a teacher or two. I think, for example, of names like B. O. Smith, Arno Bellack, Israel Scheffler, Dwight Allen, John Holt, Jules Henry, Edgar Friedenberg, and realize that there is probably not a card-carrying member of Division 15 of the APA in the group. I cannot agree that educational psychologists have a corner on taking a close and profound look at what happens in classrooms. If anything, we should be embarrassed that so many fundamental ideas presented as belonging to our field have been contributed by outsiders.

Does educational psychology consist of a body of knowledge, whatever might be its origin? Is that what we have to contribute to teachers? To some extent, I must accept this as part of the answer. We do know some things that ought to be of interest, if not value, to teachers. We can speak with certainty about the correlation between IQ and achievement, about the educational correlates of social class status, about some of the fundamental properties of learning, and so on. Yet if our contribution rested solely on what we know, we would be out of business tomorrow. One way of dramatizing this hunch is to imagine what would happen if all the solid knowledge in our field were suddenly eliminated from the minds and books in which it is contained. How far back toward a caveman status would such a catastrophe push us? I hate to admit it, but I doubt that we would have lost much ground as humans or that the state of teaching would suffer terribly in the wake of ignorance that followed.

---

1. John Dewey. The relation of theory to practice in education. In C. McMurray (Ed.), *The Third Yearbook of the National Society for the Scientific Study of Education, Part I.* Chicago, Illinois: University of Chicago Press. P. 28.

I am forced to conclude, therefore, (in a somewhat McLuhanesque manner) that facts may be our medium, but they are not our message. Our message, in my judgment, resides less in what we know than in what we believe. Accordingly, our contribution to teacher training entails, in essence, the communication of our beliefs, both overtly and covertly, to the students with whom we work. Herewith is a final pot-shot in the direction of one of the big fellows mentioned at the beginning.

Undergirding the work of most educational psychologists is an intricate system of unspoken beliefs. These hidden foundations of our thoughts and actions may not be held in conscious awareness by most of us. Yet we behave in ways that are consistent with them, and therefore, I assume that they could be explicitly revealed and affirmed. Even without our conscious consent they continue to function, giving direction and continuity to our efforts and imbuing those efforts with a meaning that transcends their public intent. Indeed, the indirect expression of these beliefs may well be the most effective way of communicating them. However we accomplish it, I suspect that the transmission of these basic ideas may well be the most important contribution we have to make to the preparation of teachers.

It has been pointed out in the earlier section that belief is a slippery concept and I have not changed my mind. Therefore, I have no hope of conveying more than a fuzzy impression of what I have in mind. Nonetheless, I would like to offer a few examples of what seem to be some fundamental commitments underlying our teaching and research. I do not contend that any of these beliefs are unique to educational psychologists. Other groups of people obviously share many of them and may even hold them with greater intensity than we do. The overall patterning of these notions may constitute a total way of thinking that differentiates psychologists from others holding similar views, but we do not know enough at this point to make such a claim.

The educational psychologist believes in the importance of education as a human enterprise. Admittedly, there is a pompous ring to this sentiment. We obviously ascribe to it, for all that we are doing would make no sense if we did not. Not only do we believe that education is important in human affairs, we also believe that the process of conducting it can be improved. If we knew all there was to know about the best ways of effecting change in ourselves and our fellow man we would have a clear conscience. We would still have the responsibility of passing our knowledge to others, but all of our research efforts would no longer be necessary. Even those among us who place a greater stake on knowledge for knowledge's sake would have to admit, I think, that the ultimate goal of our work is the improvement of the human condition.

This commitment to the benefit of man is usually combined, in psychologists, with a belief in the superiority of some methodological strategies over others. Improvement will only come, we contend, as we apply the techniques of rational analysis to the problems confronting us. We cannot simply wait for the millenium to arrive. We must do something about it. Something entails the use of imagination, systematic thought, logical analysis, and all of the other higher cognitive processes at our disposal.

Our methodological bias goes still further and includes a commitment to looking, to measuring, to counting, and other ways of assembling evidence to test the veracity of our ideas. We are, in a word, empiricists. We believe in the reality of the world outside our skins and we turn to that reality as a final judge when inconsistencies of thought require resolution. While it is true that some of us are more rigorous in our application of this belief than are others, I have never met an educational psychologist who would argue against the value of empirical evidence in instances where it can be obtained.

Because we are psychologists, rather than sociologists, anthropologists, or some other breed of social scientist, the basic unit of our analysis is usually the single organism. We may study groups of students, computing means and standard deviations as we go, but the major events in which we are interested, teaching and learning, are not performed by groups at all. They are the outcomes of individual actions or, more precisely, the actions of individuals. Therefore, it is necessary for us to worry about what is going on inside the little black boxes, even though we may never be able to open them up to take a look. This concern is reflected in the centrality, in our work, of concepts that refer to intrapsychic phenomena. Intelligence, motivation, attitudes, learning — these are terms we seem unable to dispense with, no matter how far we push our behavioristic leanings. In short, we believe that what happens inside a person is important. A deeper understanding of these hidden processes is our *raison d'être*.

As I look back over these few samples of our underlying beliefs, my confidence in our potential usefulness to teachers is greatly strengthened. Teachers too must come to believe in the importance of education, its susceptibility to rational and empirical analysis, and the dependence of its success on the internal workings of the human organism. I think we can help to bolster these convictions. Beneath the controversy a core of agreement seems to rest. The points on which we agree comprise the heart of our message, though the language in which it is communicated may continue to show great variability.

Perhaps if all of our students already shared our beliefs there would be little left for us to do. Some might argue that we would still have the task of teaching teachers exactly how to behave in classrooms. But as William James reminded us in 1894:

I say moreover that you make a great, a very great mistake, if you think that psychology, being the science of the mind's laws, is something from which you can deduce definite programmes and schemes and methods of instruction for immediate schoolroom use. Psychology is a science, and teaching is an art; and sciences never generate arts directly out of themselves. An intermediary inventive mind must make the application, by using its originality. . . .

To know psychology, therefore, is absolutely no guarantee that we shall be good teachers. To advance to that result, we must have an additional endowment altogether, a happy tact and ingenuity to tell us what definite things to say and do when the pupil is before us. That ingenuity in meeting and pursuing the pupil, that tact for the concrete situation, though they are the alpha and omega of the teacher's art, are things to which psychology cannot help us in the least. [Pp. 23-24].[2]

Here then is what comes of swatting flies. These are not the trophies I would like to have displayed to you, but at least they are proofs that I have been out in the woods. The big beasts, the ones that got away, can still be heard, baying in the distance.

Commentary

Carl Bereiter

Philip W. Jackson has asked, "What would happen if all of the solid knowledge in our field were suddenly eliminated?" The question has been raised before and there is no use clutching at straws: we all know what the overriding answer must be. The same question could be raised, however, about all the knowledge in the behavioral sciences, and, although there would then be more straws to clutch at, I think the final answer would have to be the same.

Concerning the behavioral sciences broadly, however, there is a slightly different question that requires a different answer. One can ask for instance, "How would things be different if Sigmund Freud had never lived?" I claim that things would be quite a bit different, that all of us would see the world and think somewhat differently from the way we do now and that there would be a multitude of small and possibly some large differences in the way social institutions have developed in the present century. All this is quite apart from either the solid knowledge, if any, that has emerged from psychoanalytic investigation or the beliefs held by Freudians.

To Freud, the knowledge that came from his clinical investigations was important, in that he would not likely have achieved his insights by merely speculating upon common knowledge; but once the insights were formulated they became in large measure self-obvious and confirmable in daily observation. Thus the original novel findings and the theory constructed to make sense of these findings have become less important, while the insights themselves and the manner of thinking have become a part of conventional wisdom. All thinking about human behavior has consequently been enriched and lifted irreversibly to a somewhat higher level because of them.

A classic is something that forms part of one's educational background whether one has read it or not. Accordingly we can get by, for example, without

---

2. William James. *Talks to teachers on psychology: And to students on some of life's ideals.* Introduction by Paul Woodring. New York: Norton, 1958.

teaching Freud or Dewey. Perhaps we would thereby do the students the favor of not belaboring what is for them so obvious. A recent study (Whiteman, 1967), for instance, shows teenagers of both middle and lower class to have quite a substantial intuitive grasp of the material on defense mechanisms that formed the bulk of college courses on the psychology of adjustment twenty years ago.

Educational psychology courses could therefore try to teach what is to become but is not yet classical thinking about human behavior. This calls for some prescience but not so much as might at first appear. Professors are ordinarily a generation ahead of their undergraduate students in their fields of specialization though they may be a generation behind in other respects. Consequently, thinking that is already on its way to becoming classical among the professors will not be so for the present generation of undergraduates and is likely to be missed by them unless it is taught.

For instance, I think it is becoming fairly clear that B. F. Skinner's contribution to psychological thought will be an enduring one among psychologists since it has already been thoroughly assimilated into everyday thinking. Just as Skinner is being elevated to this classical position in which his ideas are assessed and reassessed rather than actively debated, we read in *Newsweek* (ten years after the event) that he is being challenged by an upstart named Chomsky. Now, of course, educational psychology texts have been teaching about Skinner for years and students have been coming out variously believing that he is a nasty man who believes in treating children like rats or that by discovering reinforcement and getting rid of the mind he solved all learning problems.

Unfortunately new developments in thinking about human behavior, while opening new possibilities of understanding and action also provoke strong moral and dogmatic reactions pro and con. In the findings of our research (Bereiter and Freedman, 1962) education students, who tend to have a rather fundamentalist mentality anyway, are quick to interpret even the most esoteric doctrinary dispute as a battle of the good guys against the bad guys, and the issue is settled for them as soon as they have decided which are which. Although Jackson declined to discuss fully his views on belief versus knowledge, I am disturbed by the hints he dropped throughout the paper which suggest that he would favor more rather than less concern with ideological matters in the teaching of educational psychology. I see this as merely a way of producing more fanatical believers and disbelievers, more slogans and counter-slogans, more teachers who are for Piaget and against Skinner or vice versa, but who have not profited in the slightest from the work of either one.

If we acknowledge that educational psychology is in some measure improved by the works of Skinner and Piaget then ideally we should try to pass on this benefit to our students. But if this doesn't mean passing on factual knowledge or beliefs, what does it mean? To put what I said earlier more starkly, innovative thinkers such as Freud, Dewey, Skinner, and Piaget add an increment to the corporate IQ of the human species. They enable us, their cultural heirs, to be a little smarter in some respects, to be a little more perceptive, subtle, profound, or incisive in our thinking about some aspect of reality. Freud was not the first to look behind the surface of human behavior to discover hidden motives and unlikely antecedents; he readily acknowledged the priority of novelists and poets of the past. But he was the first to elaborate an art by which we less gifted folk could accomplish something of the same kind. When the theoretical dispute is cleared, we can view Skinner as a successor to Freud rather than the leader of a completely alien movement, and as one who further developed and greatly simplified Freud's art of inferring the hidden antecedents of everyday behavior.

What we should try to do is give students the increment in IQ without all the agony of belief and disbelief that hampers its coming. This is not easy, but there is a time-honored principle that is applicable to the effort. The principle is, "Should follows Can." Try in every way to get students to where they have the capability of applying a new way of thinking before putting them in a position to pass judgment upon it. It is too late to do that with Skinner; the word is out on him and many students arrive ready to do battle. But it is easy to do with Piaget, for instance.

According to the usual introduction, Piaget is a psychologist who worked all by himself for years in far-off Switzerland, where he found out about the three stages of cognitive development, only nobody would listen to him because "he didn't have any statistics." But then some Americans tested his ideas and discovered that almost everything he said was right, so now we know that children learn from experience and not from just having somebody tell them, and that learning should proceed from the concrete to the abstract, and that children all have to go through the same stages in the same order although some Americans think you can speed up the process and a lot of others say why bother. Thus we go off and running on questions about whether thought precedes language and whether intellectual development can or should be speeded up.

If we are any smarter or any better as educational psychologists for having studied Piaget and worked with his ideas, it is not to the credit of truisms or falsisms such as the above. It is because we have managed to acquire and make our own some of his art in probing children's concepts and modes of thought. Students could do this — not replicating his tests to confirm his findings, but investigating other concepts and problems in a Piagetian manner. The ardent behaviorist, who objects to Piaget's mentalistic talk can be advised to ignore it: "You can interpret it any way you like, but just go and find out as much as you can about how children explain the fact that some things cost more than others." After such training the theory is apt to come as something of an anticlimax, but no matter. Having already insured that the students will take away something worthwhile from their study of Piaget, the instructor need not hesitate when presented with the inevitable question, "What does all this tell us about how to teach?" to give the most candid answer, which is, "Nothing you don't already know." (An answer, by the way, which is about equally appropriate for every theory.)

There is every indication that the future will be stormier than the past when it comes to teaching new ways of thinking about human behavior. Many of the advances in thinking that promise to be enduring contributions to psychological intelligence have a distinct engineering flavor to them, if indeed they do not come directly from computer science. At the same time, students appear to be increasingly disposed to accept or reject everything on passionate moral grounds. Students are likely to arrive already inflamed with issues such as whether the mind can be compared to a computer, whether it is moral to "engineer" behavior, and whether the "punched card mentality" is taking over. These are issues worth discussing, but it probably ought to be done in some other course where the discussion could be in competent hands. Unless educational psychologists are willing to play the roles of third-rate philosophers in their courses, they will need to devote great ingenuity to devising ways of teaching students the newer arts of thinking about human behavior without embroiling them in crises of belief.

References

BEREITER, C., & FREEDMAN, M. B.   Fields of study and the people in them. In N. Sanford (Ed.), *The American College.* New York: Wiley, 1962. Pp. 563-596.

STERN, G.   The measurement of psychological characteristics of students and learning environments. In S. Messick and J. Ross (Eds.), *Measurement in personality and cognition.* New York: Wiley, 1962. Pp. 27-68.

WHITEMAN, M.   Children's conceptions of psychological causality. *Child Development,* 1967, **38**, 143-155.

PROGRAMS AND PROPOSALS

The Relevance of Psychology to Teaching Conceptualized as Information Processing

Frederick J. McDonald

I shall begin my analysis by stating some assumptions and making some distinctions. My first assumption is that the means by which teacher trainees learn psychology need not be confined to one or two courses in educational psychology. I think that educational psychologists have needlessly circumscribed their role in teacher training by limiting themselves to a lecture course designed to convey to trainees the nature of the field of educational psychology. I do not say that such a course has no function, but rather that the functions of psychology in teacher training should not be limited to a course and need not be mediated in the traditional course structure. My second assumption is that the teacher trainee will need to acquire his understanding of educational psychology and its application to teaching in successive stages. What these stages might be is not at all clear, because very little research has been done on the development of the teacher trainee from the inception of his training program to the time when he becomes a reasonably effective teacher.

The basic distinction I would like to make is between the problem of applying psychology to education and the problem of training teachers to utilize psychological information and skills in teaching. But first it is necessary to distinguish between the discipline of educational psychology and the practical use of psychological knowledge in modifying educational systems and inventing new ones. Educational psychology is a scientific, comprehensive study of the entire educational process. Its purpose is to discover how individuals learn under the conditions of schooling as we know them, and how the conditions of schooling might be modified to increase learning. It is concerned with such questions as what is meant by intelligence or aptitude, how aptitudes are measured, how concepts and principles are learned, how the characteristics of the teacher-student interaction affect the student's learning, and what the influence of the peer group is on the acquisition of attitudes and values.

Such questions are properly the object of scientific, disciplined inquiry and analysis which may have very little relation to what is traditionally called "teaching." Except for special purposes, the work of educational psychologists can be conducted successfully in its own right and need not be housed in schools of education. How the results of this work might best be used in the educational process is, however, a separate problem which could best be investigated by a group of professionals who could play a mediating role comparable to that of engineers. Although such a group, able to mediate between educational psychologists, teachers, and teacher educators, does not now exist, one envisions its development as a matter of practical necessity. Where and how the "psychological engineers" could best do their work they would themselves have to find out through practical experience and analysis of their new role.

The training of teachers to use psychology is a problem in its own right, distinct from the scientific inquiries of educational psychologists and from the innovations of psychological engineers. Indeed, the only aspect of this problem which is mainly the concern of educational psychologists is the question of how teachers learn or could learn to apply psychology in educational practice. This is a learning problem which can be studied like any other learning problem. But who should direct this training and how to determine the conditions under which it will occur is partly an organizational problem and partly a problem in the definition of institutional roles. We need not assume that psychologists will conduct this training, since we are not, in the strict sense, training teachers to be psychologists. The training of psychologists is properly the task of other psychologists, but the training of teachers to use psychology need not be one of the functions of psychologists.

At this point an analysis of the component problems of the more general problem is needed. I think that the failure to make the distinctions I have been making, or to attend to them, has interfered with our analysis and study of how teachers learn psychology and learn to use it. For example, I think many people assume that educational psychology would have little value in its own right. We find very few, if any, instances of educational psychology being taught as part of an undergraduate major. To me, this omission means that educational psychology is not regarded as an integral part of the discipline of psychology, which I believe it ought to be. One could also make a convincing case that educational psychology ought to be part of the liberal education of undergraduates, since many of its problems should be of interest to any intelligent and educated adult.

Another consequence of not making these distinctions is that educational psychology tends to be judged by its value to teachers and administrators. Over the years there have been many books and pamphlets that describe what educational research has to say to teachers. Anyone who has written a text in educational psychology knows the kinds of pressures that are brought to bear upon him to write for what has been uncharitably referred to as the "teachers college" market.

Similarly, the value of educational research tends to be judged by its consequences for immediate action. If the research leads to greater understanding of the educational process, but not to clear implications for modifying school programs or decision-making, it is regarded by many as worthless. Their estimate of its value is reflected in their labeling of such research as theoretical: a thinly disguised way of saying that the research has no practical value.

It seems to me that we are discussing (*a*) a scientific problem: how do teachers learn to apply psychology to education; (*b*) an engineering problem: how do we develop a system for this training. The practical consequence of attacking these two problems may be that psychologists will work very closely with teacher-training institutions and become involved in teacher-training programs. The proper role of the psychologist is, in this case, to do research on the above problems.

But this is only one possible approach. These problems may be studied in many different ways. It may be more fruitful to study either or both of these problems in unconventional settings. For example, we might learn more about how individuals learn to apply psychology to educational problems by training Peace-Corps volunteers or teachers in Head-Start programs.

One final and very arbitrary distinction remains to be made: that between teaching and instruction. I prefer to use instruction as a comprehensive category of which teaching is one component. It seems clear that the developments of the next several decades will be of such a character that many different means of instruction will be used in the schools. The most obvious development will be the use of computer-assisted instructional systems. I think it is important that the task of teaching be defined as one way of instruction significantly different from the kind of instruction provided by computer-systems and that which has historically been done by using textbooks. Unless we make some distinction of this kind, and hold a belief that the human being has a unique function, or a non-replicable one, most of this discussion would be a waste of time. We are simply polishing the bones of the dinosaur. We might more appropriately call ourselves paleontologists than psychologists.

Heuristic teaching

If it is agreed that substantial changes will be effected in the nature of schooling by the development of technological systems, then it becomes clear that we, as psychologists interested in the training of teachers, ought to commit ourselves to the development of new teaching styles. We ought to commit ourselves to the discovery of ways in which the human being as teacher can influence learning. (Obviously many of us will continue to work on the correlative task, finding ways of instructing that do not require a human being except in ancilliary roles, or where the human being is the designer of this system but not its functional component.)

At present we have little understanding of, and even less empirical data on what this teaching alternative may be. Some individuals are emotive about the uniqueness of human beings and insist that a teaching function will always remain for human beings. They provide little insight into what the nature of this function may be. One must be content, at this point, with a vague and general conception. Such a conception points to areas of inquiry and strategies for testing teaching styles which will ultimately lead to a clearer understanding of the unique roles that the human being might play in instruction.

Interestingly, the synonyms listed in Roget's *Thesaurus* for "teaching" and "instruction" are all words that convey the meaning of the didactic mode. Our label, heuristic, has several meanings, all associated with the notion of discovery and inquiry leading to discovery.

Heuristic teaching refers to styles of teaching that emphasize the development of self-initiated and self-directed learning; that stress the discovery of knowledge rather than absorbtion of it; that place the student in the role of inquirer. The heuristic mode represents any style of teaching behavior or teaching activity that is characterized by the spirit and mood of inquiry, critical skepticism, invention, imagination, and enthusiasm for learning. It represents ways of treating students as persons who can produce knowledge and understanding meaningful to themselves. It is revealed in sets of beliefs about knowledge and understanding that are integral to personal development, and to the pursuit of a meaningful existence. The heuristic approach may be the essence of the styles of those great teachers who inspired students to seek understanding for themselves.

Heuristic teaching styles in teaching will take many forms that have these common characteristics. The teacher himself will be an active inquirer, making the learning process itself a part of his act of inquiry. Teaching will be the means by which the teacher himself learns; he will be as actively engaged in learning while teaching as are his students.

He will stress openness of inquiry. He will recognize and emphasize the relativity of knowledge. He will not make arbitrary distinctions between knowledge and living; between understanding and being; between social importance and personal relevance. He will not think of teaching as giving knowledge and understanding but as helping students to seek them.

The nature of his interpersonal relations with students will also be changed. He will appeal to the authority of free inquiry rather than to the authority of persons. He will not impose his greater knowledge or deeper insight on students; rather, he will rely on their perceptions of his competence to stimulate them to seek him out as a guide.

The characteristic behaviors of students will also be varied when they are being taught with heuristic teaching styles, and will have the following common characteristics. The student will be an active inquirer for, rather than a passive recipient of, knowledge. He will see the process of learning as a way of achieving his most significant personal goals. His definition of a goal, that which will have significance and meaning for him, will emerge out of the processes of learning. He will not make an arbitrary distinction between being and learning, between personal relevance and education, between meaning and personal significance.

He will assume personal responsibility for his own learning. He will not need to be goaded to learn, for the significance of learning will have become intimately personal for him. He will view education as a means of achieving his goal. He will not see teachers as threats to his personal integrity, but as means for achieving and enhancing it.

Admittedly, these descriptions represent ideal characterizations of both teachers and students. The realists, familiar with the schools as they exist today, will despair of ever achieving a system in which there are large numbers of such teachers and students. The kinds of teachers and students described represent ideals and these ideals represent goals to be achieved.

The argument for developing, studying, and promoting the teaching style described is simply that to be human is to change and to adapt. At no time in man's history has he been called upon to be more adaptive, more changeable, more aware of, and responsive to, the wide array of forces impinging on him. He is in almost instantaneous contact with any human being with whom he wishes to communicate or who wishes to communicate with him. He belongs to many different kinds of groups, each making its own set of unique demands upon him, each requiring of him adaptation to its norms and expectations. The person who responds rigidly in these situations runs a very great risk of coping inadequately with them, of creating destructive interpersonal relations, and of developing maladaptive life styles. Man has always needed this capacity to adapt. In previous times when the pace of social and physical change was slow, when men lived relatively isolated lives, when society was more simply organized, the need for adaptation was not as great. A man could successfully live his life with the habits and principles of his father or his grandfather. In an age of accelerated change, the ability to adapt to change becomes the single most important habit or style of living required by an individual.

Although this idea is widely accepted, some of its consequences have not been recognized nor fully accepted. If the ability to adapt to complex life situations is as critical as it appears to be in this era, it is obviously important that a substantial portion of educational effort should be devoted to developing individuals who are adaptive, flexible, and inventive. That our energies are not so devoted is very clear.

Even if one is not sanguine about the development of the use of computer-assisted instruction, it is clear that the world in which we live has changed substantially because of the widespread availability of information. The child today lives in a world of information. He has only to turn on a television set, pick up a magazine or a newspaper to have more information than his grandfather may have had in a year. He has a sense of immediacy, of closeness, to events as they are transpiring. He need not imagine what people look like; he sees them on television and in pictures and magazines. Pictorial journalism, whatever the media used, has opened up to him a world of symbols and images and colors. He is inundated with information.

In such a world, how does one know what is worth knowing? The very richness of what is available forces one to choose. One must choose what to read or watch; one must choose what to remember. Such choices require standards, or values, or principles, or means to help one to decide what to select. The need to adapt is even greater than it has ever been, even if it is simply to cope with the vast array of information available to each individual.

It is important to recognize that only schools can provide a wide variety of approaches to learning. If it seems likely, as it does, that one approach to learning, namely, the passive reception of information fostered by an excessive didacticism, is likely to be enhanced and facilitated by technological development, then we must ask ourselves what the consequence of this enhancement is likely to be. Will we not facilitate the acquisition of passivity, indifference, and alienation?

That these are not unlikely outcomes seems apparent when we consider the mood of the present high school and college students. Large numbers of them are alienated from the world in which they live. Others are in active rebellion against the social system that channels them into being statistics in manpower counts rather than human beings. They are strident in their charges that the educational system is forcing upon them a way of life whose values they cannot accept. They are demanding new forms of education that must provide ways in which they can develop themselves as persons.

Implications for applying psychology to teaching

It has always been true that the way in which psychology is applied to education depends upon one's conception of what the educational process is and ought to be. The teaching and learning styles described above, should they become the dominant mode used by teachers and students, would determine both which psychological concepts and principles would be relevant to teaching, and the kinds of training programs that would be required so that teacher trainees would learn these applications. I shall propose a model of teaching and of the training process that is consistent with these styles of teaching.

It is obvious that those aspects of psychology most relevant to didactic instruction would not be relevant to teacher training, given my suppositions about the directions in which teaching, in the limited sense, should go. Psychology is obviously relevant to instruction in the broad and comprehensive sense used here.

A less obvious implication is that prospective teachers will not be required to teach what they have learned in content matter. Teachers may still learn the details of the subjects they are going to teach for their own education, but it will not be necessary to learn these items to pass them on to students. The information transmission aspect of teaching will be sharply de-emphasized.

Another implication is that changes of the character that I envision will not occur simply as a consequence of finding new ways of training teachers to use inquiry-oriented teaching styles. Changes in the organization and administration of schools are also necessary. Teaching as I have described it is not a simple exercise, nor something that is done occasionally, but an integral and major component of schooling. The consequences of teaching in this heuristic manner are unforeseen, but certainly any major shift to this mode of teaching will have massive effects on pupils, administrators, counselors, and parents. Also teacher-training institutions as they exist simply could not prepare this kind of a teacher, since they too are dominated by the didactic mode of teaching.

Finally, it is also obvious that the way in which educational psychology is taught will have to be radically revamped. I readily agree that there are parts of what is now considered to be the content of that discipline which should be taught by the didactic mode. My major proposition is that if teachers are to learn the heuristic style of teaching, educational psychology must be taught in the same manner. The subject matter of educational psychology is secondary in importance to the manner in which it is taught.

An inquiry-oriented approach to teaching educational psychology

The most relevant model of the teacher as actor in the teaching situation is an information-processing model. The components of this model are the input of the teaching experience, the output of teaching behavior, and the processing capacities of the teacher that mediate between the input and the output. Using this model requires us to ask two questions: What information is, or should be, part of the input in order to produce certain kinds of teaching behavior? And how will we conceptualize the information-processing capacities?

To answer the first question we must begin at the pupil end of the student-teacher interaction. If we assume that we need to produce in pupils the complex kinds of behaviors which I have summarily labeled inquiry-oriented behaviors, the teacher must be able to recognize these behaviors when they occur, and be able to stimulate and encourage their occurrence. The teacher must be sensitive to the ways in which students perceive the world around them, to the interpretations they are making of it, to the values they hold and the influence of these values on their observations and interpretations. The teacher must be sensitive to the difficulties students have in forming and testing their hypotheses. The teacher must be aware of the pupil's evaluation of his own knowledge, and of what knowledge means to him.

The teacher must be able to stimulate the inquiry-process by creating situations in which it is required, by rewarding it when it occurs, by understanding and being empathetic with the students engaged in inquiry. The teacher will need to know when to assist and when not to impose assistance on students. He will have to live comfortably with the disorder and slow pace at which learning seems to be occurring.

These are the complex phenonema that the teacher must be sensitive to as part of the input system, and the kinds of behaviors that must characterize the output system of this model. What assumptions must we make about the information-processing capacities of the teacher? Our description will depend upon what we consider to be the primary characteristics of the information that the teacher is receiving, and what we regard as the transformations that the teacher must make on this information.

The information received is obviously complex because it is incomplete and disorganized. That is, there is no way in which the teacher can see inside the head of the student to get information on all of the transformations that the student himself is making while engaged in problem-solving and inquiry-oriented behavior. The teacher perceives only a very small amount of the actual behavior of the student. He can only hypothesize about the covert responses that the student is making. Also he can only predict hypothetically what form or pattern the behavior of the student is likely to take. The major demand, therefore, on the teacher is to hypothesize about the meaning of his observations of pupil behavior, and about the directions that behavior might take.

Similarly, the teacher, in transforming this information, is required to predict hypothetically what the consequences of his teaching behavior will be upon the behavior of the pupil.

Therefore, the information-processing capacities most relevant to the kind of teaching described here are those that transform data into hypotheses about teaching actions, that transform information into evaluations of the effects of teaching actions, and that expedite the teacher's employment of these hypothesis-making transformations.

The teacher-student interaction in this model is conceptualized as a cybernetic system in which the teacher provides input into the information-processing system; the pupil in turn is the feedback system providing input to the teacher. Both systems are engaged primarily in hypothetical transformations that enable each to interpret the behavior of the other. The basic learning for both teacher and student is hypothesis-making and evaluating.

It should not be implied that one cannot be specific about what teaching actions to take in given teaching situations; that is, that there never will be "rules" to guide action. This is the description of a model of a process. It is a cybernetic model; its physical analogy would be the analogue computer. It derives from the psychological model described by Miller, Galanter, and Pribram in *Plans and the Structure of Behavior* (1960).

A model of the training process

Since I think in terms of information-processing models, it is obvious that I will turn to them when I wish to conceptualize the training process itself. The goal of the training with which we are most concerned is to determine how teachers learn to apply psychology to education. I prefer to elaborate that problem in terms of the following questions. How do teachers learn to think psychologically about educational processes? The general answer to this question is, how do we train teachers to inquire about education?

Can the study of education from a psychological point of view be a genuine activity in inquiry? Changing teacher-training procedures to an inquiry-oriented program requires a radical change in the viewpoint of the many teacher educators who believe that the beginning teacher needs to be told what to do so that he may succeed in his initial teaching experiences. It does not seem to have occurred to many of them that training teachers in this way shapes their conception of the nature of teaching activity. If you encourage teachers to believe that teaching is a process that can be subsumed in a few simple concepts, an activity that can be successfully conducted by applying a few rules, you effectively eliminate any possibility that they will approach teaching as a problem-solving activity, demanding the best of their personal resources.

Although it will not be a small task to change the orientation of teacher-education programs, it is not necessarily an impossible one. Further, one can hardly expect massive changes in this direction until a demonstration has been made to show that such an approach leads to more effective teaching.

The following strategies probably should characterize an inquiry-oriented program. First, such a program must be organized around the analysis of problematic experiences. The discipline of educational psychology can make a major contribution here by providing insights into problems that are most likely to evoke inquiry, and when invoked are most likely to provide understanding of the psychological aspects of educational problems. Second, the spirit and orientation of such a program must be that teaching is a problematic situation that must evoke problem-solving behavior on the part of the teacher. Third, the program must encourage hypothesis-making and hypothesis-testing.

The technology for mediating these activities is available. We have, at Stanford, utilized microteaching as a way of providing easily available experience in teaching. The microteaching format in training provides an opportunity to gather experience quickly, an experience that can be controlled in many respects. For example, a teacher can test a hypothesis about a teaching behavior and a pupil effect in a relatively short period of time, analyze the consequences of this experience, repeat the test with modifications of behavior now hypothesized to be effective, and reevaluate effects. The microteaching format for training controls many aspects of teaching experience and so enables the trainee to focus on the particular aspect of teaching he wishes to study.

We have used videotape recorders to collect data on teaching behavior, which is then used as part of the feedback process to the trainee. The feedback process can be arranged in a variety of ways. For example, an instructor can sit with the trainee and stimulate his thinking about his teaching behavior while both view the videotape recording of his teaching performance. Another variation is to have the trainee view the performance himself, raise questions about what he was accomplishing, make predictions of what he might have achieved had he performed in another way, analyze the processes that he used to arrive at certain decisions, and evaluate the effects of enacting those decisions. Trainees can be organized in groups to discuss teaching problems and the hypothetical aspects of such problems.

Thus, almost any variation on strategies for producing inquiry-oriented behavior can be stimulated by using these small capsules of experience and the technology which makes them instantaneously available for analysis. Furthermore, for example, the length of the particular teaching experience may be varied in a variety of ways.

It is obvious that the critical ingredient is not the technology of controlling teaching experience, but the kinds of problematic situations posed and the kinds of inquiry about the situations stimulated. Here we return to what is probably the basic problem — namely, that instructors must have an inquiring attitude about the nature of the educational process. This attitude, this orientation, this involvement in inquiry is the necessary condition for producing inquiry-oriented teachers. The technology is simply a device to bring experience in a form in which it can be analyzed more effectively.

This technology is also useful in providing training in specific skills or teaching behaviors. We have had considerable experience in training teachers to use some very specific skills that are components of a more complex teaching style oriented to producing inquiry-oriented students. These skills are subcomponents that must be put together in progressively more complex patterns.

A basic strategy for training teachers to be inquiry-oriented might be one in which the teachers begin with inquiry about elemental, or simple, teaching problems, move progressively through more complex problems, until they are involved in long-term inquiry-oriented experiences. The initial stages of this training may be easily provided by a perceptive use of microteaching and its associated technology.

However, it is more difficult to provide the kind of experience necessary for the total development of the teacher than the experience necessary for managing inquiry as a basic teaching style. Such experiences require field laboratories where the teacher may be involved in teaching in inquiry modes on a long-term basis. At our Research and Development Center, in 1969 we are going to create a number of field laboratories of this type. Without them, we could not begin to provide the fullness of experience necessary for the development of heuristic teaching styles.

In studying the training process we have worked mainly with two kinds of variables: modeling and feedback variables. Demonstrating a teaching behavior provides a rich opportunity for inquiry. It is not difficult to visualize extensive analysis and discussion of a teaching performance one has observed, in terms of its effects; what hypotheses the teacher probably had in engaging in certain kinds of teaching actions, what alternative hypotheses might have guided the teaching behavior, and what implicit conceptions of how individuals learn seem to be the underlying theory of the teaching strategy.

The major impact of the kinds of strategies described is that they provide an opportunity for problem-solving that demands psychological analysis of educational problems. The approach that is recommended is the opposite of the didactic approach in which we tell trainees the problems, the relevant principles to solve the problems, and in some instances the best solutions. Instead, this strategy emphasizes the activity of the student as an inquirer who defines the problem to the best of his ability, who seeks information relevant to solving it, who utilizes his personal and other resources to solve the problem, and who in the process comes to see the relevance of psychological knowledge to the solution of his educational problems. The strategy requires that we begin with the problem and work back to the relevant psychology, rather than provide the psychology and require the student to apply it.

It must be obvious that the heuristic teaching style is here recommended as the desirable mode of teaching educational psychology. I cannot prove that adopting this teaching style will produce spectacular results, that all teachers will come to know and understand the relevance of psychology in a way not previously grasped. But, if we seriously accept what we know to be true about learning, the choice of this style of teaching follows as a logical necessity.

Commentary

Fred T. Tyler

In his paper, Frederick J. McDonald dealt with questions about teaching and learning at all levels with some considerable emphasis on how we prepare teachers to apply psychological concepts in a heuristic teaching mode conceptualized as an information-processing model involving input, output, and processing — all of which involve hypothesis-making and hypothesis-testing. It is not possible to deal with all of his concepts and propositions. A few have been selected for consideration; some of these deal with his assumptions and some with his proposals.

Early in his paper McDonald states that "to be human is to change." If this be so, many of us are either subhuman or superhuman — for I find marked resistance to change on the part of many of those individuals who have been for some time engaged in the preparation of teachers. They resist change with every means at their command — and I doubt that their resistance is one of Stephen's inherited tendencies. In fact, if I may depart from my response to McDonald's paper for a moment, I should like to say that I am unable to conceive of any behaviors that are inherited — if by inherited we mean biological transmission from generation to generation. I think I can remember J. B. Stroud writing years ago that "all behavior — at least all significant behavior — is learned." However, regardless of Stroud's assertion, one has to consider for oneself what is transmitted from one generation to the next, the gene, and its contents. If we deny that "to change" is a natural, inherited tendency we are faced with a teaching-learning problem. We need to discover how to foster change.

Well then, we learn to change, or at least some of us learn not to change. There is security in stability, and to change is to lose this sense of security. Fortunately, some also learn to be attracted by the new.

Surely, McDonald is correct in saying that this ability to change is, today, of crucial importance. Does educational psychology have anything to say about the preparation of teachers who will be alert to the need to change their purposes, materials, and methods? How do we prepare teachers who will instigate change or who will at least accept change, even if they themselves do not initiate change? If educational psychology has no suggestions we should look to anthropology and sociology for we find considerable interest in these disciplines in the process of change.

Actually, I think we should have something to say about how we go about getting individuals to learn to change. However, a prospective teacher's attitude toward change is not dependent solely upon educational psychologists. It can be nurtured by the individual's contacts with other parts of the program, including practical experiences in the classroom. This places considerable burden on "student teaching." On the other hand, there are those who would virtually eliminate this aspect of the "practical" component of teacher education, believing that it provides ample opportunities for inappropriate experience and an insufficient guarantee of useful experience.

According to McDonald's position, teachers must be highly adaptive, and this type of behavior cannot be produced by didactic methods. Didacticism, supplemented by certain types of technology, he suggests, will produce passivity and indifference. The didactic approach must be replaced by other teaching styles associated with the heuristic approach if we are to avoid this passivity. However, in the next sentence he points out that today's students, taught by didactic teachers, are in open rebellion. Unless I misinterpret, didactic teaching is supposed to produce passivity and indifference but it is producing active rebellion and open concern about, not indifference to, many issues.

What is heuristic teaching? It is a style of teaching which involves self-initiated and self-directed learning in a spirit of free inquiry which emphasizes the discovery rather than the absorption of knowledge. If heuristicism is to replace didacticism, the role of the teacher must undergo a radical change; and teacher-education programs, including educational psychology, must get teachers to learn the new role. Just what will the role be? How can we prepare for it? Will we, as usual, be fifty years behind the times?

It seems that one implication of the heuristic approach is that the teacher will need less "content." He may have some if he feels a need for it as part of his own education — but he does not need it in order to function as a heuristic teacher. Is this really so? For instance, could Polyai have been a successful heuristic teacher without his knowledge of mathematics? Can we really say that teachers do not need "knowledge" when they are using the heuristic approach?

I cannot help wondering how a "contentless" teacher can carry out some of the duties assigned him in heuristic teaching. For example, how can he "recognize and emphasize the relativity of knowledge" and how can he "help students to seek knowledge and understanding" when he may be lacking in both. It is true that under these conditions he will not be able to impose his "greater knowledge" on the pupils. The emphasis on method and de-emphasis on content is also found in educational psychology. How can the teacher "stimulate the inquiry process by creating situations" unless he is well versed in suitable situations? Robert Karplus, for example, insists on teaching in the classroom just because he is so familiar with science.

With a heuristic teacher, a pupil will "assume personal responsibility for his own learning. He will not need to be goaded to learn." This does indeed sound like an ideal situation. But is it realistic to believe that each pupil can and will accept the responsibility for "appropriate learning"? What will he learn? Will it be only that which he perceives at a particular time as relevant to him without any question about learning some things of more general social importance? Will there be any reasonable sequence to his learning or will there be gaps as he jumps from one self-initiated "problem" to another? The heuristic teacher makes assumptions about human nature and the nature of knowledge. Are they justified?

McDonald recognizes that the heuristic teacher must expect disorder in his school and that he must live comfortably with the "slow pace at which learning seems to be occurring." Can all school activities be conducted in a heuristic manner? Does a pupil have all that much time? One of the other speakers talked about the excessive time we spend on our schooling. Discovery takes time. Possibly teaching should be a combination of heuristic and didactic methods. Why do we have to go from one excess to another?

I doubt that in our present stage of knowledge we can deal with the question about *"how"* we learn." Learning goes on "inside" the individual. We infer something about learning from observing or measuring performance. Tolman's latent learning experiments showed that "learning" had taken place even though there was no evidence that it had occurred until the situation provided a reason for a change in behavior. I think Jackson commented on the internalized nature of learning. McDonald does, too, when he points out that because he cannot see what is going on inside the pupil's head during inquiry-oriented behavior, the teacher has to hypothesize about the pupil's behavior and about the consequences of his teaching activities. Similarly the pupil has to make hypotheses and test them.

If the role of the teacher is to be heuristic in nature, we need to ask about the preparation of teachers. Should they be prepared by heuristic procedures, to solve problems in a self-initiated and self-sustained manner? Possibly they should, on the assumption that heuristics is good at all levels (which may or may not be true). Learning at the early ages may be facilitated by the use of objects and models; it may be more effective to illustrate "erosion" than to talk about it to second-graders. It may be more meaningful to produce for a college class a catatonic schizophrenic than to verbalize about one. And yet somewhere, we have to rely primarily upon words for teaching and instructional purposes.

McDonald urges that teachers be "trained" to "inquire about education [p. 15]," pointing out that this would require some serious surgery in teacher-education programs which, in many cases, rely upon the transferring of prescriptions and recipes from the teacher-educator's experiences to the student's notebook. Many, he says, believe that effective teaching requires simply a few well-cured, time-proven rules. If we believe this, our students will believe teaching should be prescriptive at all educational levels, from kindergarten through the professional program.

Surely McDonald is correct in saying that if we are to have heuristic teachers then teacher-education programs must change, and even more correct when he says this will be no easy task. I think he also is correct when he urges us to *demonstrate* that inquiry-oriented teaching is more effective than is didactic teaching. We can stand to have many more systematic, serious, and thorough studies of teaching-learning processes.

What can educational psychologists do that will foster heuristic teaching? First, they can organize their program around problems the answers of which would help students to understand how psychology can help in the teaching act. Where do these problems come from? Apparently at Stanford the students are able to discover their own problems through first-hand experience in their laboratories. But some of us have many more students, no laboratory, no research and development center. Direct observation in classrooms is possible, but this may be disrupting to both teachers and pupils. And there may not be many classes that are inquiry-based so that many observers would not be able to discover problems relating to heuristic teaching. Films and videotapes offer another possibility, and discussions among students may even turn up problems which can be investigated and which do reveal psychological issues. I am sure that there are at present educational psychologists who are using an inquiry-oriented, highly-individualized approach, for example, Charles G. Galloway of our faculty at the University of Victoria.

To change schooling from a didactic to a heuristic approach will not be easy. Many professors believe that they are not doing their duty by their students unless they stand up in front of them for fifty minutes three times a week for fifteen weeks — or twenty-five weeks in most Canadian universities. However, we must not think that the teacher is the only one who must change. Many pupils, despite their protestations, demand their pound of flesh be returned after it has been cut off.

When should prospective teachers study the implications of educational psychology for teaching — in their junior year or concurrently with student teaching? Or would the outcomes be more significant if they had a period of teaching before looking into educational psychology to see what it has to offer?

We have heard of the conflict between methodology and psychology, between instruction and learning; this conflict will continue as long as these are kept separate. Too often the method teachers have too little knowledge of psychology to use it effectively. Too often the educational psychologist is unaware of the potentialities of his discipline for teaching. The two types of specialists need to come to terms and work with each other. And, again there is evidence that this is happening. Methods teachers with a reasonable background in educational psychology talk psychologically about methods.

Educational psychologists are usually tied to their discipline because it is through their published research that they receive their rewards. If credit is given to their research for reasons related to other aspects of education, to the preparation of teachers, more educational psychologists will become partners in teacher education. If there is no change in what we expect of them they may wait until they are full professors at the top of the salary schedule before they become involved in educational problems.

I am in agreement with McDonald when he urges us to make more use of technological developments. This is especially so in the case of videotape recorders for observing lessons, and for microteaching. We find that teachers and students are enthusiastic; they feel no threat. We need more systematic evaluation of its effectiveness for teaching students how to apply psychological principles. I am not sure I am ready to go all the way and say, as some do, that we should substitute microteaching for first-hand experience in the classroom.

I suppose I am as pessimistic as McDonald, Ausubel, and Jackson about current educational psychology because it has not answered *all* our questions about learning. As educational psychologists we need to get busy. Education is not a matter of *translating* psychological studies into classroom methodology, as Hilgard, Postman, Spence, and Underwood have argued. They agree, however, that we need to try out psychological theories in practical situations.

And yet we may be asking for too much. As Jules Henry (1963) pointed out in *Culture Against Man*, learning is man's most difficult problem; it is one which can never be finally solved because the more culture changes the faster it changes. Our understanding of learning will always lag. Also, the cultural condition affects and modifies questions about learning and therefore answers to questions are going to change. What was appropriate in the 1930's was no longer appropriate after 1957.

In summarizing, I find that I am sympathetic with much that McDonald says. And yet certain of my interpretations, or misinterpretations, cause some concern. Can we study *how* a person learns, for example, how he learns to apply psychological concepts to the classroom? We can investigate the means by which we can facilitate learning. Learning is an individual matter; surely, it is redundant to talk about self-learning.

Just how far is McDonald willing to go in rejecting content in favor of method? Can we rely solely upon heuristic styles of teaching? Is the information-processing model, with its emphasis on hypothesizing, an appropriate description of teaching and learning? These are still questions without answers though there is much in McDonald's position that is appealing and satisfying.

Technology, Si—A Psychology of Techniques, No

Bernard R. Corman

I

I would like to assume that all teachers, elementary as well as secondary, ought to be prepared in four- or five-year university-degree programs, and that they should have a university education. The fact that this is not the case in the largest provinces of Canada makes moot the problem of our concern. For if teachers are to be stationed in classrooms after Grade 13 and a twelve-week special course in pedagogy, there is little that psychologists can do except to pass out a few prescriptions for survival and our best wishes. The relevance of psychology for teachers is a question at least as old as William James's *Talks to Teachers* (1920). James drew attention to the gap between teachers' expectations that psychology provides answers for specific classroom problems and the fundamental nature of the laws psychologists can warrant (pp. 7-20). Many of our modern colleagues, John Herbert and Donald Williams, for example, still share James's view; they insist that even today our science offers, at best, conceptual organizers to guide the teachers' analyses of problems. And many still agree with James that those psychologists who presume to offer more are either fools or frauds.

My own position has been a waffle for I am torn between my conviction that, for teachers, psychology is best conceived as a "foundations" subject, and my respect for the technology coming from our laboratories. My stance has been to support the widest possible diversity among instructors. The results of this policy can be embarrassing as in the instance of a husband and wife, enrolled in the same educational psychology course, who found they could not discuss any substantive issues. They were enrolled in different sections with different instructors. But on the whole my *laissez-faire* approach has been a comfortable one, reflecting my commitment to academic freedom.

This waffle is becoming untenable. For the salient development of our time — the emergence of an educational technology — requires a less ambiguous policy. Otherwise we, and the teachers we prepare, are likely to be overwhelmed by the changes in their functions as teachers and in their conditions of work.

The new technology is as sophisticated as Patrick Suppes' computers and as uncomplicated as E. Lakin Phillips' behavioral structuring. What is new and common in these otherwise disparate developments is the subdivision of instructional tasks into their critical components, and the bringing of organized knowledge and methods of science to bear on each sub-task and on the combination of sub-tasks. The spread of the new technology and its con-comitant effects on the culture of the classroom will be more rapid and sweeping than what can be imagined by many who are now overwhelmed by the pro-jected costs. We must remember that Wiener felt impelled to be defensive in his 1950 prediction (pp. 184-89) that servo-mechanisms would come into their own in industry in ten to twenty years. What then seemed an innovator's optimism now appears to have been undue caution. I know of no reason to expect developments to be any less swift in education. The students now in our faculties of education will have to cope with the changes that follow in the wake of an advancing technology.

II

What we, as psychologists, should be doing to help teachers cope depends on the changes we foresee. Two quite different predictions are fashionable. In the first we are told to expect changes of degree but not of function. In this forecast the teacher is expected to become his own programmer, or at least to control the choice and sequencing of instructional programs produced by others. The new devices are seen simply as additions to the teacher's toolbox (Lysaught and Williams, 1963, pp. 19-21). It is true that the source of the teacher's decisions will become the partial theories and task-related knowl-edge now being developed rather than maxims deduced from global psy-chological systems. But the teacher, although now supported by machine and human aides, will remain as the final arbiter of practice. Or, as J. D. Finn (1964) puts it, the teacher will become even more of a professional than he is now with greater need to understand learning theory and to combine effectively old and new methods (pp. 20-21).

The implications for teacher education in this first view of the future are straightforward. They call for a greater emphasis on a psychology of the technical than now exists. Gagne (as quoted in De Cecco, 1964), for example, suggests that topics such as the techniques of task analysis, the principles of component task achievement, intra-task transfer, etc., are likely to be more useful than the well-known principles of reinforcement, distribution of practice, response familiarity, and so on. Others urge that prospective teachers be given controlled practice in modeling their behavior after carefully chosen exemplars, exercises in simulated classrooms, experience in programming small instruc-tional units and in analyzing the structure of subjects in the curriculum. Given the assumption that the functions of teachers will not alter basically, these emphases and experiences are probably superior to those that are now provided. But our early experience at Alberta in developing software for computer-assisted instruction and my understanding of what John K. Galbraith (1969) calls the imperatives of technology makes me fairly certain that teachers as individuals who will remain in face-to-face and continuing contact with pupils will *not* benefit, and indeed may be penalized if these emphases do become dominant (pp. 11-21).

I also share a second view of what lies ahead, that once we are beyond the present transition period, teachers will contribute little to the production of the materials that the new technological devices will employ or to the sequencing of programs for individual pupils. For as organized knowledge is increasingly brought to bear on practical problems, the lead time between the initiation and the completion of a task progressively lengthens. In our context, the few hours teachers now take to prepare an hour's classroom activities stretch into the weeks and months required for a team of specialists to program that same hour for a computer, for a simpler teaching machine, or for a fifty-minute film. Some teachers, of course, will be absorbed into the teams of technicians now forming. But they will thereby cease to be "teachers" in my restricted sense. Organized knowledge, Galbraith points out, can be brought to bear only by those who have it, and an advancing technology inevitably proliferates specialists whose contact with the users of their products is minimal.

There is more involved here than the addition of new devices or additional constraints. System and provincial inspectors, provincial examinations, approved texts, and syllabi, and all the rest presently limit the teacher's freedom. These existing constraints are imposing but a teacher who knows what he wants to accomplish can easily circumvent them (Corman and Olmstead, 1964, pp. 57-88). The constraints that technology will introduce will be of a very different order. For these will effectively separate the teacher from an involvement with pupils in what is now central to their relationship: the joint exploration of the subjects of the curriculum. Or, as the slogan goes, the teacher will be "freed" from the drudgery of the classroom.

Two other imperatives of any technological advance make me less than sanguine that teachers will be able to use their promised freedom in productive ways, especially if their training becomes even more technical than it is at present. The first is that an advancing technology breeds greater inflexibility. Computer-assisted instruction, for example, does provide for individual differences among pupils, but these are the differences that arise in working through identical programs. Suppes (1966) reminds us of the difficulties we will face if we attempt to provide separate instructional systems for field independent and field dependent students (p. 174). And this is only one of the many basic differences among learners, which might dictate alternative instructional systems. Once fully developed instructional systems are available, fascinating school board meetings will probably ensue as decisions have to be made to spend the hundreds of thousands of dollars that a new generation of computers and computer programs will demand.

The teacher will be relatively powerless because capital investment requires that the new equipment be used by those who are technically expert in directing the work of technical experts. Briefly, the new technology brings the industrial twentieth century inside the educational establishment. There are obvious advantages: more intensive teaching than is possible by conventional instructional methods, more ready access to information, greater efficacy in learning, and greater control (Gleason, 1967, pp. 76-78). But these new advantages can seem inflexible to teachers, who feel impotent in the midst of the complex organization dictated by technology. The result is that the freedom now promised to teachers may easily turn out to be as destructive as the freedom promised to other craftsmen when machines were first installed. Obviously the current disaffection of many teachers is the indication of their reaction against the inflexibility and the powerlessness they already feel.

III

The spread of technology into education is now irreversible. In the United States, for example, NEA estimates that in 1967-68 expenditures for elementary and secondary day schools will reach 31 billion dollars and this reflects a growth rate of 10%. This is *almost* what the U.S. will spend on the Viet Nam war! The spread of technology is inevitable because an industrial state cannot really leave the intellectual development of its human resources to the individual decisions of thousands of school boards, administrators, and teachers — or even to the wisdom of professors of educational psychology.

The new breed of teachers will be many kinds of specialists. Technicians of many kinds will be needed in education, of course, and psychology will be important in preparing them. Stephen Hunka, who directs the CAI work at Alberta, tells me that even at this early stage he foresees a requirement for system analysts, system programmers, subject analysts, learning theory specialists, psycholinguists, program sequencers, specialists in the application of the psychology of perception, and electronic gadgeteers. And this is only the beginning of his list. But the psychology relevant for the training of such specialists in education is not necessarily the psychology that will be appropriate for teachers.

Given our discipline's involvement in the new technology, the probability is that a pyschology of techniques will be presented to teachers, however inappropriate it may be. Faculties of education, teachers' associations, and educational psychologists are going to have to confront the fact that classroom teaching experience is neither a necessary or even desirable prerequisite for many of the emerging specialties in education. The notion of a common preparation may have been defensible when each worker in the educational enterprise was expected to do pretty much what every other worker did. But this has not been wholly true for some time, and it will become progressively less valid.

Indeed, teachers will need to have some understanding of what is involved in the new technology. But this need will be no greater than that of other citizens of the twentieth century. It is useful to know the workings of a car, but one can drive without knowing how to raise the hood. And if my forecast of the future is even partially valid, teachers will not be the mechanics, and perhaps not even the operators of the new machines. Teachers could become little more than proctors putting tapes on and off the computers, pulling boots off and on youngsters, monitoring behavior, and the like. Or, if their associations are strong enough, teachers may become engaged in a kind of featherbedding, sitting passively in a corner while their youngsters interact busily with the computers.

The basis for a more productive function exists, however. Teachers and pupils could share aesthetic experience and engage in a joint examination of affect and values. By this I do *not* mean that teachers will offer courses in personality theory, philosophical systems, art history, and the like. This work, too, can be provided effectively by machines. I mean rather that teachers could become a countervailing force against the deadening influences of our industrial society. They could provide experiences that would help youngsters discover better alternatives than those provided by LSD, high-speed cars, the search for status, and the anaesthetic of television.

If they are to function in this way, teachers must be prepared to interact with students as authentic human personalities, and not as pseudo-machines. For, as Arthur Combs (1965) puts it, if teaching is to be a relationship between two individuals, the teacher must *be* somebody; there can be no relationship with a nonentity. As Abraham H. Maslow (1967, pp. 195-206) writes, if students are to learn who they are, how they feel, and what ideas have meaning for them, the teacher who wishes to help them must first know who he is, how he feels, and what ideas have meaning for him. A psychology of techniques is hardly likely to help teachers achieve the necessary self-understanding, or the openness and ego strength necessary to communicate with others.

There is a kind of psychology that does have relevance for this purpose which is prepared to accept as useful other methods of inquiry than those based on logical positivism, which is concerned with the ideographic as well as the nomothetic, which does not separate cognition and affect into isolated compartments, and which is concerned with human intention as well as human behavior. It is an instructive exercise to scan the indices of recent educational psychology textbooks and see how infrequently the so-called humanist psychologists (such as Frankl, Rogers, May, Fromm, Bugenthal) are cited. And yet in my own experience it is precisely these writers to whom teachers respond with excitement and interest. The rapid spread of sensitivity training groups among teachers is a concrete evidence of the appeal of this psychology. One may dismiss the teachers' interest as the response of the naive but I prefer to believe that teachers are telling us that it is a psychology that makes a difference for them. And if this is so now, it will be even more true in the future.

There are many questions that must be dealt with in defending my thesis that not one psychology but several are required in the preparation of educational workers and that the humanist point of view ought to be more widely introduced to those who will be teachers. One must ask in what sense psychology is an "educational" psychology fit for inclusion in the calendar of a Faculty of Education or, given the tenor of research on the reasons individuals choose to become teachers, whether it is realistic to urge them to assume a rebel's stance toward our industrial society. But these important issues, and many others, must be deferred since I do want to indicate in closing how the point of view I have expressed is being introduced into our work at the University of Alberta.

Those who have visited us recently know that we are actively engaged in the development of the new educational technology. Using our new computer we are developing "software" and specialists (though not yet at the undergraduate level) who will be able to take their skills into schools and into industry. We have also encouraged the development of human learning labs, including two that are applying the psychology of perception to the problems of instruction.

But at the same time we are fostering "humanistic" approaches in our work with teachers. This year our graduate students have experienced a "basic encounter" group. The early results suggest that it is possible to cut away some of the ritual and rigidities in which graduate study in education is now embedded. At the undergraduate level we are experimenting with the small groups that accompany our large lecture sections so that students will be free to examine affect and reflect on how, among other things, it "feels" to become a teacher.

In another instance two of our undergraduate instructors have broken with the lecture system. They meet small groups of students half-an-hour each week, set problems for them in the psychology of learning, and then free them to collect data and analyze it as groups.

In one final experiment a staff member is working with a team. No formal course in psychology is offered but students are provided with experiences in schools which serve as data for their and the staff's joint analysis and interpretation.

None of these efforts is startlingly new but each is an attempt to provide a more human interaction between staff and students in the face of large enrollments. I cite these groping efforts not because they are successful but only to make the point that psychologists can be more than the midwives of the new technology. Psychologists are creating their own kind of atom bomb for teachers; they should also take up the challenge of dealing with the consequences of their ingenuity.

References

COMBS, A. Teachers too are individuals. In Don E. Hamachek (Ed.), *The self in growth, teaching and learning: Selected readings.* Engelwood Cliffs, N.J.: Prentice-Hall, 1965. Pp. 457-461.

CORMAN, B. R., & OLMSTED, A. G. *The internship in the preparation of elementary school teachers.* East Lansing, Mich.: Michigan State University, 1964.

FINN, J. D. Teaching machines: Auto-instructional devices for the teacher. In J. P. De Cecco (Ed.), *Educational technology: Readings in programmed instruction.* New York: Holt, Rinehart and Winston, 1964. Pp. 20-21.

GALBRAITH, J. K.   *The new industrial state.* Boston: Houghton Mifflin, 1967.

GLEASON, G. T.   *The theory and nature of independent learning.* Scranton, Pa.: International Textbook Co., 1967.

JAMES, W.   *Talks to teachers on psychology and to students on some of life's ideals.* New York: H. Holt & Co., 1914.

LYSAUGHT, J. P., & WILLIAMS, C. M.   *A guide to programmed instruction.* New York: John Wiley and Sons, 1963. Pp. 19-21.

MASLOW, A. H.   Isomorphic interrelationships between knower and known. In F. W. Matson & M. Ashley (Eds.), *The human dialogue: Perspectives on communication.* New York: The Free Press, 1967. Pp. 195-206.

PHILLIPS, E. L., & WIENER, D. N.   *Short-term psychotherapy and structured behavior change.* New York: McGraw-Hill, 1966.

SUPPES, P.   The uses of computers in education. In Scientific American (Eds.), *Information.* San Francisco: W. H. Freeman, 1966. Pp. 157-174.

WIENER, N.   *The human use of human beings: Cybernetics and society.* Boston: Houghton Mifflin, 1950.

A Psychology Course Planned for the 1968 Harvard-Newton Summer School

Maurice Belanger

For the past twelve years the Harvard Graduate School of Education in colla-boration with the city of Newton, Massachusetts, has sponsored a six-week summer school for elementary and junior high school pupils. The Harvard-Newton Summer School also serves as a clinical facility to introduce interns in the Master of Arts in Teaching Program to the study of education and to practice teaching. During the morning portion of the Summer School, interns under the supervision of a master teacher plan lessons, teach and subsequently conduct an analysis of the teaching session. In the afternoon interns take a psychology course offered by one or more Harvard staff members. The psy-chology course has varied a great deal from summer to summer depending on the particular instructor giving the course, but in general, it is fair to say that the course has been quite traditional in content and presentation. Intern reaction to the psychology course has been mixed, but two general criticisms seem to have been quite standard from year to year. One criticism has been that the course has little or no direct relation to the morning program; a second criticism often made was that the course was of questionable relevance for a beginning teacher.

In the summer of 1967 several changes in the Harvard-Newton program were made, and the plans for 1968 are a revision and extension of the work begun in 1967. Before proceeding to describe the changes planned for both the morning and afternoon portions of the Harvard-Newton Program, a few general comments related to the education of future teachers will serve as background to our current thinking.

One fact that teacher trainers too often fail to take into consideration is that a beginning education student already knows a great deal about teaching and learning before taking any formal course work in these areas. The student has, after all been observing teachers for a long time, sixteen years in the case of our interns. He knows what school is like for that's where he has spent most of his life. In no other professional area does a student enter with a greater number of preconceived ideas about the nature of the work of the professional. He has been a learner in school and will now leave the student chair and cross over to the other side of the desk. This transition is by no means an easy one as can be attested by the initial teaching performances of interns. Early lessons range all the way from rigid script-like lessons to loose contentless "happenings."

Regardless of the particular style of teaching carried out, the student teacher is nevertheless operating on the basis of a conception or model of teaching.

The purpose of the Harvard-Newton Summer School, as we are beginning to reconceive it, is to provide a clinical setting where the intern can make more explicit his model of teaching, examine it, have it challenged, modify and remodify it on the basis of knowledge and experience. In past years rather than starting with the intern's conception of teaching, we at Harvard-Newton have probably been too enamored with our own conceptions, our own knowledge, and even our own wisdom. The teacher trainer, of whatever variety, has built up his own complex model of teaching and learning over a period of many years. It is not surprising, therefore, that attempts to communicate directly items that are selected from this rich collection often fail to be assimilated into the intern's own model and are rejected as trivial and useless. What we know can be of service to the intern if we focus not on the attempt to use this knowledge to shape the intern's model to be congruent with our own, but rather on what the intern now knows and believes about teaching and learning, and use our knowledge to help him evolve more complex, rational, and effective models. Although a teacher-training institution can provide contexts where the initial process of personal reformulation can be accelerated, yet the process continues during an individual's total career. Teaching is a personal invention, and part of "being a professional" means constant reinvention.

Thus, at Harvard-Newton 1968 different contexts will be provided in which the intern can examine his assumptions about teaching and learning and put them into practice. Harvard-Newton programs prior to 1967 have essentially provided one conceptual mode of the teaching-learning process, the one most prevalent in schools. In the summer of 1968 rather than one mode three will be utilized. Now what are some of the modes in which a person learns? The three selected shall be referred to simply as Modes One, Two and Three in the following brief descriptions.

Mode One is the most familiar of all and can be described in terms of four major components. One component can be considered as being represented by the "Library of Congress," i.e., the accumulation of the *known* codified in signs and symbols. From this vast domain one selects a minute portion to be arranged in a second component — the school curriculum. The persons who are to receive the knowledge, the students, and an agent of transmission make up the two remaining components. The agent could be a programmed booklet, a computer, or a teacher. Essentially the mode is designed to transmit or communicate meaningful samplings of the known. If one thinks of school today, the events that take place in the classroom, the role of the teacher, curriculum, evaluation, teacher training — in fact, thinks of the entire educational enterprise — we might be led to believe that this mode is *the* only viable structure for learning. There is no question that it is a viable mode for learning, but recently a group, labeled the "romantic critics," has been calling attention to some defects as Mode One is practiced in many situations. The recent books by Peter Schrag,

Jonathan Kozol, Herbert Kohl, John Holt and Philip Jackson indicate dramatically that Mode One as operating in some cases can have many negative attributes. Mode One forms of school are long overdue for a penetrating re-examination. The romantic critics are performing a valuable service by reminding us that the ultimate test of all our claims, philosophical and psychological, rests on what actually does or does not happen to children in school.

Since Harvard interns think of school largely in terms of Mode One, we wish to provide opportunities to have them examine their own assumptions. Some of our students see only the positive aspect in Mode One and these only in a narrow sense. Many interns see themselves in the teaching role as mini-scholars. Having just spent four hard years assimilating a few bookshelves from the Library of Congress they are now prepared to spread the good news. The intern often needs to reexamine his discipline, to view his discipline in a new way if he is to make it meaningful to students. In the area of teacher training in science, for example, it is notorious that science majors from excellent universities haven't the foggiest notion that science is a human enterprise and not, to use Schwab's term, a rhetoric of conclusions. The mini-scholar intern needs desperately to be placed in confrontation with teen-agers and children in situations other than formal didactic instruction to enable him to see them as people in their own right, and not necessarily as potential future mini-scholars to be fashioned in his own image.

But mini-scholars are not the only types of interns today. There are an increasing number of students who prefer action over reflection, action over knowledge, action over abstraction, action over communication, action above all else. These students see little of value in Mode One organization. How does one get such students to see the positive aspects of Mode One? By engaging in more Mode One teaching ourselves? I suspect not. We have to listen a great deal more to the contemporary student; he wants to talk with adults not be talked at by adults. But "talking with" also implies periods of "listening to." We increasingly need the two directions of dialogue, and less one way preaching. In the summer of 1968 we want to establish small groups of seven or eight interns to talk with a staff member and with each other. We hope to be able to engage in honest discourse about the meaning of being a teacher in our present society. In such sessions we anticipate that the interns will be able to examine the ideas of other interns and staff members, and juxtapose them with their own ideas. The groups will be composed of interns from a variety of disciplines so that the mathematics intern might contrast his ideas with those of a social science intern, or an English intern. But in addition we would want the intern to engage in dialogue with his own pupils. Thus, in the morning program, a part of the school time will be devoted to small group sessions of four or five pupils in dialogue with the intern. Hopefully, these sessions will not be tutorials on subject matter, but we are going to leave open to the intern the choice of content of discourse. The small group discussions are for us another mode of teaching and learning. One might prefer to characterize these sessions as group process but here they will be referred to simply as Mode Two. Mode Two is another form for learning and not just information transmission to four or five students instead of twenty-five or thirty. By characterizing them as different structures for learning, the contrasts between the two modes will hopefully be sharpened, and thus, bring into more explicit relief different assumptions upon which each mode is based.

There remains a third mode of learning, but it is a view that is quite difficult to grasp. Even the advocates of this mode of learning have difficulty trying to make explicit their own beliefs and assumptions. The characterization of Mode Three can ultimately be based on a particular philosophical stance regarding the nature of subject-object interaction. A few concrete illustrations may illustrate the nature of this interaction. Consider a child interacting with Dienes's mathematics material or with Stern's blocks, or Cuisinaire's rods. In these situations the child is not acting on some objects in a random way, and the consequence of his action provides information back to the child. In this type of learning situation there is an active dialectic between the person and the external objects. The outcome is a gradual evolution in the behavior of the person in a situation *where he is his own agent.* In Mode One there is an external agent in the book, program, or teacher, and in Mode Two there are other persons as agents, but in Mode Three the agent is the person himself. By being his own agent the person selects the objects, examines the range of possible actions, chooses an action to try out on the object, and is acted upon by the result of the action. In such cases "to know" is the outcome of actions *on* and reactions *from* objects. However, it is the rare American school that is built on the basis of this Third Mode. Many schools in British primary education, however, reflect this position. Representative are a number of schools in Leicestershire County and elsewhere in England. At present there are many indications that there will be an increasing number of elementary schools emerging in the next decade that will try to work out in practice the numerous educational implications of this third conception of learning and knowledge.

In the 1968 Harvard-Newton Summer School, we plan to have two "Leicestershire-type" classes, one for 5- to 6-year-olds and one for 10- to 11-year-olds. Both classes will be supervised by teachers experienced in this mode. While interns will not be student teachers in these classes we plan to maximize the opportunities for observation by Video-taping as many classes as possible and to make these recordings available for viewing. Thus Mode Three will be represented in the morning program by the presence of these two classes, but how do we represent Mode Three in the afternoon program? One possible conception is that the entire Harvard-Newton program is the confrontation experience for the intern. In a sense the whole program is his "Leicestershire class." What the staff needs to do is to provide the student with sufficient variety to enable him to see alternatives, to make decisions and choices, to act and to see that the consequences are the ultimate criteria for judging his action. By seeing classes organized in three modes we expect that interns will be able to see, presented in practice, a laboratory for examining his beliefs and knowledge concerning the role of the teacher, the conceptualization of knowledge, the nature of children and learning, curriculum structures, and procedures of evaluation. In summary, thus far, each mode will be represented in the morning and afternoon program. In the morning each intern will function as teacher in Modes One and Two, and as an observer of Mode Three. In the various parts of the afternoon program each intern will function at different times as a student in the three modes.

We plan to use three afternoons a week for the psychology course, although "course" does not seem to be the correct word here. On Tuesday afternoon there will be a large group lecture for all interns, and on Wednesday they will be divided into twelve tutorial groups to discuss the Tuesday lecture. On Thursday afternoon the interns will be divided into twelve groups, these discussion groups consisting of another permutation combination of the students. The purpose of the second group will be for open discussion on any matters that the participants propose to discuss. It is this small discussion group meeting that we visualize as the occasion for small group dialogue, and not for more didactic teaching.

We plan, at the moment, to have four lecture sessions each followed by a tutorial. These four sessions are to be conducted in the Mode One form with one of the staff members conducting the session. The four sessions we have in mind will deal with the following areas.

Area One (First week)   The first session will present a detailed examination of Mode One. We will select specific philosophical and psychological assumptions underlying this mode and examine their educational implications in terms of curriculum, teaching, learning, and evaluation. Both positive and negative implications will be presented.

Area Two (Second week)   Two case studies by Joseph Grannis of Teacher's College, Columbia, will be presented. The cases are published as "Monograph One" by the Research and Development Center at Harvard Graduate School of Education. Grannis will spend two days with us to present the cases. The material deals with two boys who have different conceptual styles of learning. By studying the cases, the interns will be able to see in a dramatic and specific way what the professors are talking about when they use the term "individual differences." The cases also illustrate the use of a rich variety of techniques and instruments for studying children. In the next four-week period each intern is to prepare cases on two of his own pupils. The case will be prepared with the help and guidance of the intern's master teacher and the psychology staff.

Area Three (Third week)   In this week we will attempt to modify one of the most tenacious assumptions held by our interns, namely the view that children are miniature adults. Interns tend to think of children as being quantitatively different from adults on similar categories. For example, children are seen as less intelligent and adults have more of "it," whatever "it" may be. The fact that intelligence in a child may be qualitatively different is difficult for our interns to grasp. In the past I have used illustrations from the work of Piaget to illustrate some qualitative differences in children's thinking. Both inexperienced and experienced teachers seem to get a sense of shock when they realize that children are different in quite fundamental ways. We would encourage interns to try out clinical interviews with a few of their pupils concerning subject areas they are teaching the children in the morning.

Area Four (Fourth week)   The program in this week will be based on some recent work done at Harvard. Two of my colleagues have been conducting intensive interviews with high school students trying to ascertain their perception of school and of the major adults in the school. The students interviewed have come from different socio-economic levels and attend schools in communities also of different socio-economic levels. Interviews have been conducted with students in public and private schools. Each intern has his own perception of school, but, in addition, he has a particular perception of the student's perception of school. How well do they match? Are they in conflict? The answer depends, of course, on which intern, and which high school student, but I think when the recent work of Mosher and Sprinthall is published all of us will be in for some surprises. By presenting some of this material we hope to confront the perceptions of the adolescents with those of the interns.

The foregoing statement of intention may serve to indicate the broad framework of the course. Briefly, rather than presenting a formal didatic course, four educational psychologists will be staff members in the clinical setting of the Harvard-Newton Summer Program, and will be immersed in the teacher-preparation program. Such an arrangement may aid in bridging the gap between psychological theory and the work of the teacher in the classroom.

Commentary

John Herbert

The two preceding thought-provoking papers remind me of my own early experiences of teaching. Like some of the Alberta teachers B. R. Corman mentioned, I taught without any professional preparation, both before entering the university and after receiving a bachelor's degree. My performance in the classroom probably was not very different from the behavior of some of the new interns in Maurice Belanger's program at Harvard. I taught my pupils in the way I had been taught when I was at school. I told them, assigned work to them, graded them, and threatened or praised them as I had seen my teachers do.

The result was a performance that satisfied the headmaster; but I knew that something was wrong. I decided that I needed more academic knowledge and applied for entrance to London University. But when I returned to teaching equipped with a B.Sc., I found that I still could not transform myself into a professional teacher. One may remember Alexander Pope's comment on critics in his *Essay on Criticism*:

> Yet if we look more closely we shall find
> Most have the seeds of judgment in their mind.

The seeds of judgment were there, but they needed more fertile ground; so I joined the teacher-preparation program at the Institute of Education of London University. Contrary to what almost every paper here suggests, I found it one of the most stimulating intellectual experiences of my academic career and I here express my gratitude to the teachers in that program. Philip Jackson would have found there that thought was more honored than research or writing.

The program involved cooperation among people from diverse disciplines, frequent dialogue between faculty and students, opportunities for observation and experimentation with the translation of educational ideas into classroom practice, with help yet with relative impunity. There were lectures on psychology, seminars on the teaching of school subjects, and periods of student teaching. Too often, these components in teacher-preparation programs are isolated. At the Institute of Education, integration was achieved by agreement on the importance of the intellectual life of all students at each stage of their development, and on the suitability of curriculum to their interests. The program helped me to clarify and change my values and to develop a completely different style of teaching.

There are resemblances between my early experiences and the much more condensed sequence of the three modes of teaching to which Belanger proposes to expose the Harvard interns. It might be said that at first I taught in Mode One, that at the Institute I was taught in Mode Two, and that as a result I learned to teach in Mode Three. But the differences are important. During my first years of teaching I might, to some observers, have looked like an actor reading lines, or like a programmed transmitter of knowledge. However, I did not feel that way, nor was I seeking to be a mini-scholar but rather wanting to meet the demands of a new ego-threatening situation, confronted as I was by my students. Dominating all was the continual engagement of one's personality, the need to respond immediately and correctly to the unforeseen actions of children.

Similarly, though the program at the Institute was very personal and though much of the work was undertaken in small groups and cooperatively, it was not Mode Two. Communication was not about group process but about academic subject matter, about the nature and development of the child, and about the use of arts and crafts in teaching or the variability of intelligence test scores between testing and retesting. The style of teaching I learned at the Institute twenty years ago has become increasingly common in England and is beginning to receive recognition in the United States. Belanger mentioned the difficulty of describing this open style, which is based on an awareness of the variety of ways in which children learn and develop. I have seen his paper in several different forms, a result of the experimental nature of the program which is still being formed and I am sure he did not mean to limit Mode Three to actions on and reactions from objects.

Perhaps the three modes described by Belanger are not ways of teaching so much as types of teachers — stock characters, almost. There is the teacher who teaches subject matter without regard for his audience. There is the teacher who teaches pupils without regard for the subject matter. And there is the teacher who creates an environment where students may learn to teach themselves. Yet he wishes his interns to free themselves of stereotyped conceptions of teaching, to choose appropriately among diverse alternatives, to develop a range of teaching styles and to know for what purpose or purposes each might be suitable. We might suggest ways in which this process might be supported by psychological principles and descriptive techniques.

The program at Harvard, like the one in London and a great many programs in the United States and Canada, is intended to prepare the professional teacher. Corman rejects such programs on the ground that technology and the power of industry will soon make such teachers obsolete. I hope Corman will reconsider. Over the last twenty years there have been many innovations, but no great changes in the schools. In the foreseeable future I believe we will need professionals as well as technologists, but if we cease to improve programs for the professionals, their predicted demise could become a self-fulfilling prophecy. My own recollections of my "sense of powerlessness" to effect controlled changes in my teaching, before I returned for training, makes me value the opportunity for teachers to become more professional and more aware of alternative ways of teaching.

This does not mean we should neglect the need to design different programs for the different groups of teachers Corman has described. In the schools we will need some relatively powerless auxiliaries to technology and to the students. Let us not just call these baby-sitters or gadgeteers or machine minders, and let us also not confuse them with professional teachers. They are teacher aides, technicians, secretaries, or hygienists who are able to take over tasks with which the professional should not be burdened. Let us insist that the auxiliary workers should be carefully selected and trained for their task, better than their counterparts in business and industry who need psychological knowledge less because they are not as often in contact with sensitive human beings in their phase of rapid development. If we cannot give them psychological training, however, we must make sure that they know that they lack this knowledge. Quintilian, writing in the first century, said this: "In the case of the *paedagogi* (attendants) this further point should be insisted upon, that they be either thoroughly educated — and this I should like to be the first consideration — or else aware of their lack of education [lest they be] . . . filled with a false idea of their own knowledge . . . [and] impart their own folly to their charges."[1]

Corman points out that in addition to teachers and attendants we will also need technical specialists to prepare software for the computer. It is most interesting that Alberta has a program for the preparation of such staff. We will need a specialized psychology for the designers of educational materials, but we will also need a psychology of the classroom, so that technical specialists

---

1. *Quintilian on Education,* trans. by William M. Smail, Oxford, Oxford University Press, 1938, p. 13.

and classroom teachers will be sophisticated in the ways of teaching as well as in the ways of hardware, so that they can consider the human context as well as the technological one. Though it is essential when planning training experiences to make a conceptual separation of the two kinds of psychology, and though some of the preparation of the different types of staff members for schools must be separate, I hope that in the actual programs of preparation the technologists will share many experiences with the teachers and not live in another world.

The same reservation applies to Corman's suggestion that classroom teachers might be distinguished from technical specialists through a concern with affect and with social and aesthetic value. But surely value and feeling must be *in* the educative process — whether that process be an interaction with live or electronic teachers, the learning of a foreign language, the mastering of a mathematical idea, or the discovery of the implications of a poetic metaphor. To abstract affect and value from the knowledge to be purveyed by the machine would indeed be to give way to what Corman calls the "deadening influences of our industrial society." For this reason it is of urgent importance that teachers and producers of course materials should also learn to identify and foster aesthetic and human values in the subjects and disciplines they teach. Otherwise, in accepting the new technology for education we may find that we have also accepted the delusion that we can "customize" or "personalize" the standardized product.

Thus we may well find that the psychological preparation we wish to offer to people who will perform the various functions Corman has described will differ in degree and emphasis rather than in substance, that there will have to be a core of common experiences and shared understanding. When the question arises how this is to be achieved, the two programs presented and the one proposed by Frederick McDonald are worth close examination. In presenting the intentions of the Harvard-Newton Summer School, a six-week period was considered a model for programs everywhere and a vital part of the MAT program there. Belanger has stressed that the program is still being developed. For a more complete understanding, of course, we would need to know about the rest of the program and how the summer period fits into the total year. We would also need a more precise and inclusive description of the modes of teaching to which interns are to be exposed. Perhaps the use of some systematic technique for analyzing classroom events during the summer school would not only contribute to the development of the psychological aspects of the program but would also be useful in the evaluation of changes in the students' teaching during the course of their internship year. Follow-up studies similar to the one we are conducting at Reed College could provide information about students' views of the impact of the program on their teaching, and could provide interesting comparisons.

In the title of his paper Corman asserts: "Technology Si — Psychology of Techniques, No." I would propose neither a psychology of technology nor of techniques, but rather a psychology of ways of teaching, a range of possible content and procedures designed for a variety of teaching roles. I deliberately use the phrase "ways of teaching" because it seems likely that in future we will want to examine many ways of teaching other than the giving of lessons, now almost the only way current in schools. Perhaps this collection of papers can be influential in initiating a study of what psychological knowledge is most worth teaching to all who have to cooperate to create desirable educational programs: the professional teachers, technical specialists, auxiliaries, administrators, and even school board members and governors.

Reflections: October 1968

Maurice Belanger, Kiyo Morimoto,
Ralph Mosher, Charles Rathbone,
Bernard Seideman, and *Norman Sprinthall*

It would hardly seem valid to assess the impact of the 1968 Harvard-Newton Summer School just two months after its closing, but at least we can offer some reflections on our collective experience. Independently written comments were drafted by each of the course instructors: Norman Sprinthall, Kiyo Morimoto, Ralph Mosher, Bernard Seideman, and Maurice Belanger. The course assistant, Charles Rathbone, prepared a longer commentary using materials submitted by the instructors. Drawing from these various documents, the present statement indicates our collective appraisal of the course — its single parts as well as its overall design. It also intends to give the reader some indication of where we feel the design was or was not effective, and to indicate some of the factors involved in the actual operation of the course as related to our perceptions of its successes or failures.

The first fact to be noted is the unexpected and overwhelming diversity of students represented at Harvard-Newton this summer. Out of some two hundred interns, we estimate that nearly one-fourth were "activists," more oriented toward action than rational analysis. Skeptical of the efficacy of schools and of the "Establishment" (including psychologists) that supports existing educational programs, these activists are alienated from the disciplines and generally see little of real worth in their own subject major to communicate to their pupils. Whereas five years ago an English major, for example, would argue that Beowulf to Joyce is the relevant curriculum, the current activist would construe as *the* crucial curriculum that quality of interpersonal relationship, the agape, between teacher and pupil and between pupil and pupil. Particularly sensitive to the country's social ills, these students are hopeful of changing society by changing the schools. In the meantime they show moral anguish, identification with minority groups (particularly black children in ghetto schools), guilt about being white and over-advantaged, and disenchantment with both the schools and the society as they now exist.

Half of the students appeared to belong more in the tradition of the "mini-scholar" where the discipline is seen as a major focus of interest. But even for these students one notices a strong shift towards the value of interpersonal relationship. For example, students in mathematics and science seemed particularly interested in constructing individual laboratory experiences where pupils would conduct their own investigations, or would work in small groups collaborating on some inquiry. In many cases the nature of the interpersonal relationship seemed more valuable than the actual subject content of the activity.

Over the summer we were continually discovering yet other types of interns. While the vast majority came to Harvard-Newton to learn about teaching, there were those who readily admitted they were there to avoid the draft. Another group, also small in number, were there hoping to communicate to pupils the great and fundamental ideas of western culture; to them the activists' teaching-as-happening was appalling. Though unorganized during the summer, this group has been attempting to consolidate this fall to form a group of "Basic Educators" in the tradition of Robert Hutchins and Mortimer Adler. There was a group of black interns, too, keenly involved in racial matters both in and out of the summer school; their concern and work with black pupils brought in from Boston was particularly impressive. With this incredibly complex student body it is small wonder that their reception of and reaction to our "course" was varied.

Naturally we tended to hear a great deal of commentary about the course from the more vocal student critics, and no doubt our reactions (and over-reactions) frequently tended to be based on this source of information. Our overall rating for the course would be to term it a *qualified* success, its victories not as great as we would have wished, but its failures not as pervasive as its critics would imply. To be more specific, we shall comment on the various components of the course. Each component has its own particular strengths and deficiencies.

Case studies

One of the formal assignments in the course was the preparation of case studies. Each intern group (four or five interns working with a master teacher) was to write up a case study based on two pupils in the school. In the second week of the course, two afternoons were devoted to the presentation of a sample case prepared by Dr. Joseph Grannis. Included in the demonstration was the use of a variety of instruments and techniques for gathering data (Kohlberg Moral Dilemmas Interview, Wallach-Kogan Test, indepth interviews recorded on video tape, the Stanford-Binet, etc.). In general, the initial assignment was met with very little enthusiasm by the interns, but as weeks went by, each intern group became more and more involved as they studied the two pupils they had chosen. In the early weeks there was considerable reaction against the use of formal tests; in fact, there was opposition to the notion of measurement of any person by any means. For example, knowledge of anything as fuzzy as IQ, they claimed, could only be used *against* the children. It was as though they totally rejected these forms of information and it made them feel angry to think of the unprotected youngsters being "taken advantage of" by "authorities." As the interns struggled to understand the children they were studying, their acceptance of these means increased. Facing the problem of communicating to someone else what an individual child was like, they began searching for techniques, for means to accomplish this purpose. Some intern groups invented such techniques as reading a part of a short story to a child and asking the child how it might come out, and subsequently comparing the responses from different children. In general, the interns reported at the end of the program that the preparation of the case studies was one of the most valued experiences of the summer. Some intern groups had picked two children whom they thought were very much alike, only to discover that in reality the children differed profoundly along many dimensions; others had the opposite experience, finding common characteristics in apparently dissimilar youngsters.

The psychologists teaching the course spent considerable time working with intern groups, discussing means for gathering information, the interpretation of data, characteristics of children at a particular age level, and so on. One of the stronger aspects of our model lies in this involvement of psychologists talking with interns on matters dealing with the children they are teaching every day. The realities of school are strong inducements toward helping the interns realize the value of psychological theory as a means for interpreting and making sense out of phenomena which otherwise would be seen as merely puzzling or not be observed at all.

Small groups

At the end of the summer the interns wrote evaluations of their small group experiences, and the vast majority reported positive feelings about their involvement in this aspect of the program. Especially attracted were the "new" interns — the activists arriving fresh from the turmoil of undergraduate colleges throughout the country. Disillusioned with their own experience in academia, they found the contentless nature of the small groups particularly appealing. For other interns, too, the small groups were a challenge — though many reported being both frightened and attracted by the experience. Many found themselves upset, frustrated, angry, and confused in their initial contacts with the children. To the degree that the framework of "school" was absent, having no classroom props, no predesignated curriculum, no generalized method for proceeding, the interns were thrown back to their own personal resources, their own beliefs and values.

Of course, the small group experiences were not universally successful. A few interns never overcame the frustrations of their initial encounters with the pupils; and theirs were six weeks of failure. They became baby-sitters, resorting to non-productive games to fill up the time. These interns felt that more traditional teaching in Mode One would have been more beneficial. Others felt that they already knew what children were like and that the small group experience was unnecessary and repetitious. But those who succeeded were pleased to find unexpected strengths in themselves. They established a greater variety of relations with children than the classroom setting ordinarily permits, and thus became aware of new modes of teaching and learning.

Lectures and tutorial groups

Each of our individual reports indicates dissatisfaction both with the lectures and with the tutorial groups in which the material presented in the lectures was supposed to be discussed. Attendance at the lectures decreased over the summer and by the end less than half the interns were showing up. Simultaneously, attendance at the tutorial groups also fell off. Again the ancient problem of relevance plagued us. While it was our intention to present material that was helpful to the interns, we apparently still have a long way to go toward identifying which material, and what manner of presentation, the interns will find useful. Many of the intellectual and professional issues raised in the lectures may have come too soon in the interns' experience for their relevance to have been entirely clear. The same material presented after experience in the classroom rather than concurrent with the first experience, might go much further in being meaningful. For the action-oriented students such information was not seen as useful: sitting down to discuss and explore the issues we provided was considered by them as a waste of time. Often the same material we attempted to present in lectures would emerge in our meetings with interns on the case studies. On these occasions whatever information we possessed was seen as valuable to them because it tied in with something they wanted to understand. Quite possibly the lectures could be eliminated and the material "taught" in the context of actual problems which the interns face in their work with the pupils.

Discussion groups

In order to assess the impact of the Thursday afternoon discussion groups we are forced to consider the mundane affairs of management and scheduling. These discussion groups, intended as the afternoon Mode Two experience for interns, were designed as opportunities for the interns to carry out some meaningful exploration, to probe their own attitudes and assumptions about learning and teaching within an interpersonal group context, and hopefully to come to terms with their assumptions and beliefs as they examined their sense of commitment to teaching. We hoped they would ask such questions as "How do I see myself as a teacher?", "What resources are available to me when I enter a room as a teacher?", "What psychological climates promote learning?", "Which climates inhibit?", and the like. For those who continued to come to these group discussions, the experience — by their own testimony — proved valuable. But many did drop out, and this we feel stemmed from the fact that the second meeting — crucial for continuity — was canceled, because the day fell on a holiday (July 4th). This meant that there was a two-week gap before meeting for a second session, and to complicate things still further we had an administrative mix-up about the time of meetings. Given the fact that this sort of group discussion requires considerable commitment of time and energy, and that we had available a mere seven weeks, these scheduling difficulties doomed us from the start. Tutorial group-type activities require delicacy of handling, and we fumbled badly. It takes time to develop a climate conducive to personal exploration; this we failed to provide.

The other major factor, important in accounting for the general disappointment with these discussion groups, is attributable to the activities of the master teacher and his group of interns. There was considerable time available in the morning part of the program for the master teacher and interns to discuss matters other than the particular teaching conducted by the interns. Because so little time was actually spent by the intern in teaching, he had little data on which to base the kind of discussion that might lead to an extended supervisory relationship. Much of the morning time was available therefore for discussion of a variety of issues including those we thought would be appropriate for the Thursday session. As a consequence, by the time Thursday afternoon came around many of the interns had simply exhausted the topics for discussion.

Thesis

At both the beginning and end of the summer, each intern was asked to set down in one or two pages his "theses of education," his personal credo — where he stood in regard to what education is about, what schools are for, etc. Numerous interns indicated that they found this valuable and we feel this is so because the theses required them to formulate in writing just where they were in respect to their own learning. Without a specific assignment to undertake this task they might never have had the opportunity to put the Harvard-Newton experience in perspective. These theses we feel were important and successful marks made by the interns on their own yardsticks. We hope over the academic year to attempt some kind of content analysis of these theses to serve as an indicator of modification of beliefs and values over the seven-week period.

Reading list: the course bibliography

At the beginning of the course we provided a three-page bibliography of books and articles, including the so-called "Romantic Critics" (Holt, Kozol, Kohl, Goodman, etc.), some of the psychological literature on childhood and adolescence (Friedenberg, Coleman, Anna Freud, Erikson, Kohlberg), reports on the "Integrated Day" or "Leicestershire" movement in British Primary Education (Featherstone, Yeomans, Kallet, the *Plowden Report*), as well as some sociologists' and anthropologists' writings on education (Benedict, Becker, Jackson, Henry, Thelen, etc.). Significantly, the authors read most by the interns were the "Romantic Critics."

Mode Three

It was "romantic" on our part to consider the entire Harvard-Newton context as representing the interns' Mode Three experience. In addition we felt that it was necessary to provide explicit contact with Mode Three classrooms. Our intention was to provide two demonstration classrooms, one with second- and third-graders, the other with fifth- and sixth-graders, and each with its own

British-trained, thoroughly experienced teacher. Such an undertaking had built-in risks, since the children were new to this type of classroom and we knew it would take time for the children to acclimatize to such a dramatic change of "school." Nevertheless, we did provide such demonstration classes. For the first three weeks there was little to demonstrate, but gradually many of the children did become sufficiently used to this new set of expectations so that interns could visit these classrooms first as observers and then as participants. Like so many others attempting these changes we also experienced difficulties with parents, and a number of children were transferred at the request of parents to more traditional classrooms. We again fumbled badly in not having advised the parents of what was going on, and if we ever undertake such a venture again we know we would want to have extensive contacts with the parents beforehand.

Because the two demonstration classes were placed in the middle of a fairly traditional school organization, we experienced many "administrative" difficulties antithetical to Mode Three learning. There was not only a lack of support in supplying materials but of moral support as well.

General comments

Perhaps after so many negative comments one might wonder if we would ever attempt such a venture again based on the same model. Our answer is "Yes!" Many of the problems we faced stemmed from our own ineptitude in managerial matters and from encountering difficulties we had not anticipated. First, we had not anticipated the particular variety of interns in the program, and we too often made assumptions about their needs and interests based on our own preconceptions of who they were and what they were like, not on the reality before us. In any planning for a future summer program we would certainly be conscious of the "new students" and might indeed err in being over-conscious of this group to the neglect of the others. Secondly, we now realize that it is very important to provide a much more thorough orientation of our "course," both to the interns and to the master teachers. Harvard-Newton now has a fairly long tradition concerning the role of the master teacher, and our design modifies that role to a greater extent than we realized beforehand. In the design of 1968 the master teacher plays a central, in fact pivotal role as a colleague. Because he meets with the interns in planning the courses they will teach, in planning day-to-day lessons as well as meeting with the interns after the experience of teaching, the master teacher becomes the central focal point of communication in the whole Harvard-Newton program. He turns out to be, therefore, the central supervisor for the intern and a colleague. During the past summer many questions were raised, for example, about the small groups. It turned out that the master teachers were as much in the dark about this as were the interns themselves. In many ways the master teachers' own sense of lack of direction and orientation left them unavailable as supports for the interns and contributed to the interns' anxieties. The interns have enough anxieties in just facing the problems of initial teaching without our providing still additional and unnecessary sources of difficulties. The whole area of our working and collaborating with master teachers needs to be drastically improved.

Transferability of the model

In our reflections we have tried to be candid about how we feel concerning our summer experience and the model upon which that experience centered. Our comments are parochial because the operational characteristics of the general model are intimately related to the situational factors of the particular context of the Harvard-Newton program. However, we are willing to hazard two assertions based on our experience:

(*a*) The essential purpose of our model is to provide structures exhibiting various sets of beliefs and values about teaching and learning. These are characterized by our "modes." We believe that the interns did grasp the essential differences inherent in each mode. The three modes form a useful scheme and could probably be utilized in other contexts as an organizational framework.

(*b*) Perhaps the most easily transportable factor to other contexts is the involvement of psychologists working *in situ* with beginning teachers. If we were forced to select an item as "most satisfactory" this would be our choice. Working with the interns in a school setting, the psychologist can introduce relevant psychological, epistemological, and educational thought with regard to ways of organizing for instruction and learning, child and adolescent development, individual and group dynamics, etc. Our reservations about the formal lectures, the small groups, the lack of systematic content, while representing real deficiencies, nonetheless seem secondary to the central fact that the course instructors were seen as relevant and helpful when working with groups of interns on real problems confronted by them.

We will continue to struggle with our own situational problems. At the moment our only advice to other educational psychologists is that they leap into the thick of the battle constructing conceptual modes of learning on the one hand and work directly with beginning teachers on the other. We feel that the only honest way to face the complicated world of teaching is to combine the theoretical approach with the practical.

THE FUTURE

Salient Issues from the Group Discussions

The participants who served as recorders for the group discussions at the conference were invited to report on the issues that arose. Their comments are summarized in the paragraphs following.[1]

Bryan Dockrell observed that difficulties in communication hindered the examination of fundamental issues raised by those who presented papers. The chief reason for this seems to have been the wide range in the participants' backgrounds and interests.

On the one hand was an exchange between psychologists developing new programs; on the other was a concern with the transmission of these programs to a wider public. While both kinds of participation are necessary, in future it might be useful to separate them. This conference can be considered to be for the purpose of an exchange between specialists in educational psychology. The papers presented here could be used as basic reading for a succeeding conference held for the purpose of communicating with educators and related directly to their interests.

Frank Peters also found that basic differences in outlook existed. These made more complex the discussion of three major questions that could not be resolved: how to approach psychology when it is in fact not one discipline but many; how to assess "good" teaching and "good" education; and whether there are enough ties between psychology and education for the people who are in these fields to work together. While these questions tended to inhibit meaningful discussion, progress could be made if psychologists and educators were to concentrate on issues that are of concern to both, such as whether benign "shaping," or conditioning, of man is desirable and possible.

The discussions reported on by Michael Orme focused on a consideration of recent developments in psychology that promise to bridge the distance between the behavioral sciences and education, such as programming, sensitivity training, behavioral modification, task analysis, and the preparation of cybernetic models for research in teacher training and the teaching of educational psychology. It was generally agreed that the traditional lecture-discussion format, which has been shown to be less effective than exposure to teaching models and guidance based on the learner's own performance, often inhibits the application of

---

1. The full text of the recorders' reports may be obtained from The Conference Office, The Ontario Institute for Studies in Education, 102 Bloor Street West, Toronto, Ontario.

117

psychology in teacher-training courses, and that more effort should be made to build educational psychology "lab" experiences into them. The ensuing discussions centered on the implications of educational technology as a source of new tools and methodologies for improving teacher training and on the question of whether educational psychology should be viewed as a pure science whose findings are of only indirect relevance to education, or as a discrete applied science that can yield definite programs, schemes, and methods of instruction that are of immediate value to the teacher.

In their comments on the conference papers and group discussions, Sister Frederica and Wilfred Wees dealt with the relevance of educational psychology to teacher preparation. They observe that the failure of teachers to see how educational psychology relates to classroom practice in the past has probably been due as much to the inflexibility of educational traditions as to the failure of psychology to sell its own product. In recent years, however, educational structures have become more pliant and educators have become less concerned with the external application of the disciplines than with the child's building of disciplinary structures within himself. This shift in emphasis has meant that "willy-nilly, psychology and education are becoming relevant to each other."

Joseph Grannis noted so many diverse recurrent themes in the discussions he attended that it is particularly difficult to summarize his report. To mention some of the issues he raised: Should the educational psychology curriculum stress skills, complex cognitive behavior, or attitude development? Should the emphasis be on process rather than on substance? Should its clientele include in-service teachers, curriculum specialists, and administrators, as well as teachers-in-training? Should educational psychologists think of these practitioners as clients or as co-workers? And just how willing are teachers to experiment in the classroom, and how much freedom do they have to do so? The view was expressed repeatedly that psychological theory should be applicable to educational practice, but with few clues as to what this implied for the formulation of theory and educational research. The school context of learning and teaching is certainly much too complex to permit the direct translation of explanatory theory into rules of practice. Prediction in psychological research has mainly been to confirm explanations, but without a knowledge of the rules which govern them. Should we conceptualize information processing more like bicycle riding or learning the use of one's mother tongue which are learned without knowing the rules, or more like the action of the physicist applying his model to reality? Much more needs to be done at future meetings in the way of considering what advances in knowledge about human behavior are worth imparting to teachers and what manner of training is necessary to make these advances functional parts of their thinking.

While there may not always have been agreement at the conference, definite progress was made toward solving some of the major issues in Frank Harper's opinion. One of the issues concerned the role of the educational psychologist, which can be seen as that of information-giver, scientist, or researcher.

"Ideally," contends Harper, "the educational psychologist would play all three roles at once, varying the emphasis depending on what is demanded and the setting in which he finds himself. In practice, he has tended to concentrate on the role of information-giver . . . ." Another important issue concerned the question of how the educational psychologist should teach. Dissatisfaction with didactic lecture-type methods was general, but in the papers presented at the conference only two specific proposals were made for changes: McDonald's "heuristics," involving self-initiated and self-directed learning, and Belanger's "Mode Three," which does away with the instructor altogether. There was also the issue of where the educational psychologist should teach. Some felt the educational psychologist is most effective when working closely with the teacher in the school setting, where he can see at first hand the problems with which the teacher has to deal and be on hand as a resource person. Others felt the educational psychologist is better working in a university setting, where he can retain his objectivity and have the time and resources to work at solutions. The suggestion made at the conference that he could do both may partly resolve this issue.

If the hard-nosed reappraisal of educational psychology at this conference is any indication of the future, Frank Harper affirms, its future looks good. There is need for further knowledge about learning and the educational process, a body of dedicated men anxious to fill that need, and an increasing share of research funds available. As a result, it has a greater potential for advancement than ever before; it remains to convert that potential into action.

Improving Teacher Preparation: Suggestions for Action

John Herbert

To make psychology really effective in the preparation of teachers it will be necessary, in the long run, to resolve fundamental questions about the future of the schools, the role of the teacher, and the discipline of educational psychology. In raising such questions and in offering their sharply divergent answers, the authors here have made it clear that long-range solutions are not yet possible.

Many of the papers, however, propose innovations or describe existing programs designed to achieve immediate objectives, thus showing their authors' concern with action as well as with basic issues. Action, too, was the prevailing concern of the delegates to the conference, who met in formal and informal groups to identify urgent areas for effort and suggest future steps to be taken. Their suggestions were reported by group recorders and compiled in a document prepared by a committee under the chairmanship of Evan Keislar. From this document and the group reports, as well as from the present collection of papers, there emerges a multitude of diverse proposals, expressed with varying degrees of explicitness and generality, about what should be done soon to improve teacher preparation.

By sorting and abstracting these proposals, it is possible to formulate a set of immediate or intermediate goals each of which would find many supporters. The following five seem to have widest acceptance, greatest urgency, and constitute, in effect, the recommendations of the conference: to establish regular channels for communication of research in teacher education and to foster better understanding and cooperation between psychologists and teacher educators; to develop programs to prepare professionals who can translate psychological theory into classroom practice, and assist in the building of theory by providing feedback from practical applications; to design and prepare curriculum materials for use in the training of teachers; to develop differentiated programs for teachers of different student populations and to provide a group of professionals skilled in designing such programs; and to investigate standards and resources necessary for adequate teacher preparation with a view to advising legislatures and departments of education.

Better communication

The need most frequently and strongly expressed was for better liaison and communication across professions, regions, and institutions among all those interested in the psychological component of teacher education. The problem

120

is threefold: no organization or periodical exists in this field; opportunities to meet are rare, and results of research and curriculum development are not available; and members of different groups find it difficult to communicate when they do meet.

Since the conference, the ERIC Clearinghouse on Teacher Preparation, proposed by the NEA in Washington, has become active and will no doubt facilitate distribution of materials. But other organizations are needed to encourage the production of materials and curricula in teacher education, to encourage research and publication of results, and to sponsor meetings.

This need was implicit in the report prepared by Keislar. Most of the proposals gathered by this committee were suggestions for meetings to build on the work of the conference and in turn be a resource for future meetings: a second conference based on this one, symposia modeled on the one held at the 1967 Annual Meeting of the AERA, and meetings arranged to suit the needs of a particular region or group of participants. Concerned about materials to be used at such conferences, the committee recommended that the conference report should be published and the movies made of the speakers should also be made available, at a charge, to conference participants and other interested groups. It also recommended that participants be asked to report on the use to which they put the conference results. Other suggestions were for the distribution of short pamphlets and sixteen mm. movies describing a number of pioneering programs, for a casebook on good ideas and practices, and for a clearinghouse to make these and other materials easily available.

Conference participants also expressed a need for more effective communication among different groups concerned with psychology in teacher preparation. Paradoxically, the conference pointed up this need even while it seemed to satisfy it. Psychologists, teacher educators, and teacher representatives did in fact assemble at one of the busiest times of the year, remain to the end of the last debate on a Saturday night, and participate in small group and large group discussions. Nevertheless, some members of each profession said that they had encountered obstacles to free exchange of ideas with members of other professions; and one of the nine discussion groups reported that its effectiveness had been destroyed by the same obstacles.

The cause would seem to lie in a lack of information and sensitivity to differences in roles, responsibilities, and prestige and reward systems of different professions. We know that attitudes accepted as neutral by one group are often seen as hostile by the other. Teacher-preparation staff members, faced by the immediate problems of preparing large numbers of students, want help very soon. The long-range plans and indirect procedures of psychologists seem to them to be unrealistic and based on ignorance of actual conditions in schools and teachers colleges. They assume, sometimes unjustly, that psychologists fail to visit schools or observe teaching. They may also be unaware of the pressures that lead psychologists to speak in the current technical language or to be preoccupied with obtaining publishable results from their studies. Psychologists, on the other hand, are often insensitive to the problems of teacher-preparation programs and the needs of teachers. They expect cooperation from overworked staff members and teachers who receive no rewards for participating in their researches. They arouse the hostility of teachers still further when, in their anxiety for scientific precision and rigor, they refuse to give any advice at all relating to research findings or psychological theory.

Professional interpreters

A number of participants in the conference suggested that the need for better communication could be filled by trained professionals who could mediate between teachers, teacher educators, and psychologists; translate psychological principles into classroom practice; and interpret classroom need to the psychologists.

There are several ways of looking at this role. One may see it in some way analogous to the task performed by engineers when they link physical science to industrial production. The "pedagogical engineer" would be responsible for the design, development, and maintenance of curricula, and instructional components in the schools or in professional programs. He would be in close touch with operating programs in schools and would trace the causes of problems. Since he would be there from the beginning he could also find and create opportunities for new programs. One may on the other hand see the functions of the mediating professional as analogous to those brokers, salesmen, agents, and consultants of agricultural agencies, industrial companies, and publishing houses, whose main duty is the dissemination of new knowledge to people in the field, but who often have considerable technical know-how and may do some product development. Alternatively, one may see this task as akin to that of the clinical professor in medical school, who is involved in advanced research in his field but whose main responsibility is communicating this work and other aspects of his field to professionals in training.

These new professionals would have the task of formulating a praxeological discipline from rules and knowledge derived from psychological theory, pedagogical practice, and the academic disciplines, and to force some changes in some parts of the discipline of psychology. They would require a type of training program and reward system different from those which are now applied to psychologists or teachers. One valuable training procedure might be to attach the "pedagogical engineers" to curriculum projects in teacher preparation, or to special joint university and school-district teams engaged in designing programs for the in-service training of experienced teachers.

Curriculum development

Another goal implied in the suggestions of many delegates is the development of small- and medium-scale curriculum projects to formulate materials or plan experiences for the use of teacher education faculties. On the question of whether we are ready to initiate a major curriculum project in psychology for teacher education, opinion of the delegates was divided, though some argued strongly that such a program ought to be initiated at once.

In addition to improving teacher-preparation programs, curriculum projects, whatever their scope, would provide a training ground for people learning to translate psychological theory and academic subject matter into classroom practice and place teaching acts within a theoretical framework. The procedures for initiating projects are by now well known from other subject fields. Materials developed in this way could be tried out experimentally by small groups in teacher-preparation programs.

Differentiation of programs

In several discussion groups, delegates showed particular concern with the over-crowding of training facilities and the continued existence of sub-standard programs through which low-calibre people may enter the profession without adequate screening or training. A major cause and consequence of this problem is the high dropout rate among teachers, especially in the first years of service. Badly prepared teachers are unable to cope with the difficulties of their work, and so they leave. To supply the schools with the large crop of new teachers required each year, training institutions overstrain their facilities and authorities issue emergency credentials. Can educational psychology help to break this vicious circle?

One contribution that some delegates considered was the design of differentiated programs, beyond the conventional separation of elementary and secondary teacher preparation, for people entering with different levels of education or ability, aiming at different levels of competence, or intending to perform different functions or to work with different student populations and in different regions. In the questions they raised about conference papers, moreover, many participants called for further examination of the implications for teacher training and the retention of new teachers of the increasing differentiation of teaching roles. One discussion group in particular raised a large number of questions of this kind. Here are some examples from the report of the group recorder, David Hunt (the names in parentheses are those of the authors of the papers which gave rise to the questions):

> Under conditions of rapid technological advance, how can the job specification of the teacher be made explicit? If lecturing produces only didactic learning, how do you account for the "Mode Three" effect of the conference speakers and respondents who used the didactic approach? (Belanger). Are heuristic and didactic learning operationally distinct? (F. McDonald). How are the principles of classroom learning to be co-ordinated with specific content areas? (Ausubel, Hudgins, Robinson). What are the implications for teacher training of the reported dropout rate in the U.S. of 40-50% during the first two years of teaching? What is the role of the trainee's belief system or pre-existing "theory of learning" in the induction of teaching skills? If the teacher will eventually settle into a single comfortable style, is it worthwhile to attempt to produce different modes or non-dogmatic views of certain skills? (Bereiter, Jackson, F. McDonald, Stephens).[1]

1. Recorder's report. (Unpublished)

Social and political context

The last and most controversial question is what responsibility psychologists and teacher-preparation staffs ought to assume for the improvement of the social and political contexts of teacher education. Some delegates argued, and others seemed to accept this, that they must take the initiative in informing legislators and departments of education about new programs and facilities that are needed to cope with problems such as the shortage of able candidates and the high rate of teacher dropout. In the absence of such advice, forcefully expressed, authorities are not likely to give as much weight to pedagogical and psychological factors as to financial and administrative considerations. Yet they have the power to control admission procedures, length of programs, resources available, and the staffing of teacher-preparation programs.

The officials of departments of education and of certification bureaus do increasingly realize the need for institutions to plan their own programs in order to adjust to the rapidly changing needs of society. But the resources available to most institutions for planning and experiment are grossly inadequate. Advisory groups of psychologists, teachers, and teacher-preparation people can do much to influence the allocation of resources. Some of these already exist, for example in Oregon.

Summary

Agreement on long-range goals is not yet near. Speakers and delegates held sharply opposed views on such large issues as the reform of the disciplines of educational psychology, teacher education, pedagogy, the future roles of schools, teachers, and teacher-preparation programs. Nevertheless, as has been stated, there was some agreement on medium-term goals which, if attained, will advance the solutions to fundamental problems. Five of these permit immediate action and have been discussed here: improvement of communication; development of a new group of professionals to mediate between psychologists and teachers and translate theory into practice; institution of medium-sized curriculum projects in teacher preparation; planning of more effectively differentiated programs of teacher education; and a study of the possibility of forming professional advisory groups to keep local and national officials informed of the needs of teacher education.

CONTRIBUTORS

David Ausubel

Head, Doctoral Program in Educational Psychology, City University of New York. 1966-68 Professor of Psychology and Education, The Ontario Institute for Studies in Education. Author of *The psychology of meaningful verbal learning:*

An introduction to school learning (1963) and *Educational psychology: A cognitive view* (1968).

Maurice Belanger

Assistant Professor of Education, Harvard Graduate School of Education. 1966-67 Post-doctoral grant for study and research under Jean Piaget and Barbel Inhelder at The International Center for Genetic Epistemology.

Carl Bereiter

Professor of Applied Psychology, The Ontario Institute for Studies in Education. 1965-67 Professor of Special Education, Institute for Research on Exceptional Children, University of Illinois. Co-author of *Teaching disadvantaged children in the preschool* (1966) and author of *Arithmetic and mathematics* (1968).

L. B. Birch

Professor of Educational Psychology and Chairman of the Division of Graduate Studies, McGill University. 1952-67 Senior Lecturer in Educational Psychology and Deputy Director, Institute of Education, University of Sheffield. 1961-67 Editor of the *British Journal of Educational Psychology* and author of *Teaching educational psychology in training colleges for teachers* (1962).

Bernard Corman

Professor of Educational Psychology and Chairman, Department of Educational Psychology, University of Alberta, Edmonton. 1960-66 Research Director of Student-Teacher Education Project, Michigan State University. Co-author of *The internship in the preparation of elementary school teachers: A description and analysis of a program* (1965).

John Herbert

Associate Professor of Curriculum and Instruction, The Ontario Institute for Studies in Education. 1964-67 Associate Professor of Education and Director of Master of Arts in Teaching Program, Reed College. Co-author of *Wireless observation* (1964) and author of *A system for analyzing lessons* (1967).

Philip W. Jackson

Simon Visiting Professor, University of Manchester. 1955-68 Professor of Education and of Human Development and Principal, Laboratory Nursery

School, University of Chicago. Author of *Life in classrooms* (1968) and *The teacher and the machine* (1968).

R. W. B. Jackson

Professor of Education and Director, The Ontario Institute for Studies in Education. 1957-65 Director of the Department of Educational Research, University of Toronto. Co-author of *Modern statistical methods: Descriptive and inductive* (1959) and author of *Educational research in Canada today and tomorrow* (1961).

Frederick J. McDonald

Associate Dean for Instruction and Research, School of Education, New York University. 1966-68 Director of Heuristic Teaching Program, Stanford Center for Research and Development in Teaching and Professor of Education and Psychology, Stanford University. Author of *Educational psychology* (1965) and co-author of *Training effects of feedback and modeling procedures on teaching performance* (1967).

John Macdonald

Professor of Education and Chairman of the Department of Education, Sir George Williams University. 1962-66 Associate Professor of Educational Psychology, University of Alberta, Edmonton. Co-author of *Understanding yourself and your society* (1962) and *The discernible teacher* (1968).

Floyd G. Robinson

Devoting his full time to writing. 1965-67 Professor of Educational Theory and Chairman, Department of Applied Psychology, The Ontario Institute for Studies in Education. Author of *Educational research in Canada* (1965) and co-author of *School learning: An introduction to educational psychology* (1969).

J. M. Stephens

Professor Emeritus of Education and Psychology, Johns Hopkins University, active service, 1930-65. 1966-68 Visiting Professor of Education, University of British Columbia. Author of *The psychology of classroom learning* (1965) and *The process of schooling: A psychological examination* (1967).

Fred T. Tyler

Professor of Education and Psychology and Dean of Education, University of Victoria. 1948-65 Professor of Education and Associate Dean, University of California, Berkeley. Author of *The prediction of student teaching success from personality inventories* (1954). Chairman of the Sixty-first Yearbook Committee of the National Society for the Study of Education and primary author of Part One, *Individualizing instruction* (1962).

Donald Williams

Assistant Professor of Higher Education, University of Washington. 1968-69 Assistant Professor of Higher Education, University of Illinois. Co-author of *A short history of American higher education* (in press).

Reflections and Reports

Bryan Dockrell

Professor of Applied Psychology, Chairman of the Department of Special Education and Director of the Educational Clinic, The Ontario Institute for Studies in Education. 1963-67 Director of the Educational Clinic, University of Alberta, Edmonton.

Sister Frederica

Graduate student, Department of Educational Theory, University of Toronto. 1966-68 Coordinator of Curriculum and Inspector, Metropolitan Separate School Board of Toronto.

Joseph Grannis

Director, Institute of Pedagogical Studies, Teachers College, Columbia University. 1965-67 Assistant Professor, Harvard Graduate School of Education. Author of *Case studies of children's thinking about social phenomena* (1967).

Frank Harper

Associate Professor of Psychology, Althouse College of Education, University of Western Ontario. 1961-65 Assistant Professor, Institute of Child Development, University of Minnesota.

Kiyo Morimoto

Lecturer in Education and Associate Director, Bureau of Study Counsel, Harvard Graduate School of Education.

Ralph Mosher

Research Associate in Education and Counselor to Programs in Teaching, Harvard Graduate School of Education.

Michael Orme

Associate Professor of Education, Indiana University. 1966-68 Assistant Professor, Harvard Graduate School of Education. Co-author of *Behavior modification and transfer in an out-of-control classroom* (1968).

Frank Peters

Professor of Education, State University of New York, Stony Brook. 1956-62 Associate Professor of Psychology, Ohio State University. Co-author of *The use of academic prediction scales for counseling and selecting college students* (1961).

Charles Rathbone

Completing the requirements for a Ph.D in Education, Harvard Graduate School of Education.

Norman Sprinthall

Lecturer in Education and Director of Apprentice Counseling, Harvard Graduate School of Education.

Wilfred R. Wees

Associate Professor and Head, Liaison Section, Office of Development, The Ontario Institute for Studies in Education. 1947-68 Vice-President and General Manager, Textbook Division, W. J. Gage Ltd. Author of *The way ahead* (1967).